NORTHWEST
Readers

OTHER TITLES IN THE NORTHWEST REPRINTS SERIES
SERIES EDITOR: ROBERT J. FRANK

Badger and Coyote Were Neighbors: Melville Jacobs on Northwest Indian Myths and Tales, edited by William R. Seaburg and Pamela T. Amoss

A Richer Harvest: The Literature of Work in the Pacific Northwest, edited by Craig Wollner and W. Tracy Dillon

Wood Works: The Life and Writings of Charles Erskine Scott Wood, edited by Edwin Bingham and Tim Barnes

THE

Collected Poems

OF

Hazel Hall

edited by
John Witte

Oregon State University Press
Corvallis

Substantial gifts from the following donors
helped make publication of this book possible.
The Oregon State University Press
is grateful for their support.

The Wyss Foundation
The Oregon Humanities Center
at the University of Oregon
Office of the Vice Provost, University of Oregon

Library of Congress Cataloging-in-Publication Data
Hall, Hazel, 1886-1924
  [Poems]
  The collected poems of Hazel Hall / edited by John Witte
  p. cm.
  ISBN 0-87071-478-3 (alk. paper)
  I. Witte, John, 1948- II. Title.

PS3515.A343 A17 2000
811'.52–dc21   99-089309

Oregon State University Press
101 Waldo Hall
Corvallis OR 97331-6407
541-737-3166 • fax 541-737-3170
http://osu.orst.edu/dept/press

Series Preface

In 1990 the Oregon State University Press issued its first two books in the Northwest Reprint Series, *Oregon Detour* by Nard Jones, and *Nehalem Tillamook Tales*, edited by Melville Jacobs. Since then, the series has reissued a range of books by Northwest writers, both fiction and nonfiction, making available again works of well-known and lesser-known writers.

As the series developed, we realized that we did not always want to reissue a complete work; instead we wanted to present selections from the works of a single author or selections from a number of writers organized around a unifying theme. Oregon State University Press, then, has decided to start a new series, the Northwest Readers Series.

The reasons for the Northwest Readers Series are the same as for the Northwest Reprint Series: "In works by Northwest writers, we get to know about the place where we live, about each other, and about our history and culture."

RJF

Acknowledgements

The editor wishes to extend his thanks to Karen Ford for a timely nudge that got this project under way, to Deb Casey for her close readings and insights that have kept the work on course, and to Ann Applegarth for her editorial assistance. Any admirer of Hazel Hall's poems must gratefully acknowledge the Oregon Cultural Heritage Commission and its tireless efforts to keep the memory of this writer and her achievement alive. Finally, for their generous support, the editor wishes to thank Steve Shankman and the Oregon Humanities Center, and Sandy Morgan and the Center for the Study of Women in Society, both at the University of Oregon.

Contents

Introduction xv

Curtains
Part One: Curtains
Frames 2
June Night 3
Sun Glamour 3
The World's Voice 4
Seasons 5
Footsteps 6
To a Door 7
Floor of a Room 8
The Hand-Glass 9
Silence 10
Things That Grow 11
Stairways 12
Night Silence 13
Counterpanes 14
Passers-by 15
Late Winter 16
Because of Jonquils 16
Unseen 17
Company 18
A Child Dancing 18
Roads 19
The Room Upstairs 20
The Proud Steed 21
Songs for Dreams 21
Nobody Passes 22
Shadows 23
Twilight 24
Ecstasy 25
Captive 26
Cowardice 27
Before Thought 28

Shadow-Bound 28
A Falling Star 29
Feet 30
Flash 31
Echoes 32
Loneliness 33
Sunlight Through a Window 34
Record 35
My Song 35
The Grey Veil 36
The Answer 37
Hours 37
The Circle 38
Defeat 39
The Impartial Giver 40
Sands 41

Part Two: Needlework
Knitting Needles 42
Stitches 45
Monograms 46
Late Hours 48
Mending 49
Bead Work 50
Seams 51
Finished To-Night 52
A Baby's Dress 53
Cross-Stitch 54
Plain Sewing 55
Sewing Hands 55
Lingerie 56
Filet Crochet 57
Heavy Threads 58
Buttonholes 59
Puzzled Stitches 60
Summer Sewing 61
Habit 62
Paths 62
Ripping 63

Made of Crêpe de Chine 64
Measurements 65
Instruction 66
Then the Wind Blew 66
My Needle's Thread 67
Two Sewing 68
The Listening Macaws 69
The Long Day 70
Inanimate 71
After Embroidering 71
Three Songs for Sewing 72
Late Sewing 74

Part Three: Spring from a Window
Blossom-Time 75
In April 76
When There Is April 77
Foreboding 78

Walkers
A Boy Went By 80
A Very Old Woman 81
Destinations 82
Three Girls 83
On the Street 84
Youth 85
Disputed Tread 86
Walkers at Dusk 87
The Way She Walks 88
Masks 89
A Child on the Street 90
A Late Passer 91
Shawled 91
Moving Snow 92
Ahead of Him 93
A Whistler in the Night 94
Sighers 94
At the Corner 95
Crowds 96

Walking 97
The Singing 99
A Passer 99
Pursuit 100
A Good Walker 101
Middle-Aged 102
Profit 103
More Than Sound 103
Stranger 104
He Went By 105
And Either Way 105
Nakedness 106
April Again 106
To an Experienced Walker 107
New Spring 108
He Ran Past 109
Maturity 110
Footfalls 111
The Patrician 117
Incidental 118
An Old Man's Walk 119
The Flower of Illusion 120
A Man Goes By 121
Where Others Walk 122
Bracken 122
October Window 123
Ephemera 124
The Hurrier 125
He Walked On 125
Arraigned 126
To One Coming in Sight 127
Echoes of Her 127
The Hippity-Hopper 128
Epitaph for a Neighbor 130
Today 131
As She Passes 131
They Will Come 132
Prayer Against Triteness 133
The Pity of It 134

His Eyes Are on the Ground 135
Self Inquisition 136
Pedestrian 136
The Thin Door 137
Protection 138
He Walks with His Chin in the Air 139
Apathy 140
Walker of Night 140
Sanity 141
Songs To Be Said While Walking 142
Through the Rain 143
These Who Pass 144
Hunger 145
To an Unpleased Passer 146
They Who Walk in Moonlight 147
Summary 148

Cry of Time

Cry of Time 150
Here Comes the Thief 151
To an Indolent Woman 152
Bird at Dawn 153
Before Quiet 153
Hand in Sunlight 154
Audience to Poet 155
The Ravelling Tune 156
To a Poet Who Said Too Much 157
Admonition Before Grief 158
White Branches 159
A Child Is Lost 159
Your Audience 160
Blue Hills 162
White Day's Death 162
Inheritance 163
For a Broken Needle 164
Wild Geese 164
To All Quiet Persons 165
Incantation 167
The Sea 168

Inland 169
Weeper in the Dark 170
October Chorus 171
Winter Rest 172
He Walked on Leaves 173
Incontinence 175
Pleasantry 175
The Dubious Self 176
Health 176
Light Sleep 177
Heat 178
Eleventh Month 178
Intelligence 179
Rain 180
Tomorrow's Adventure 181
Of One Dead 181
Sleep 182
Experienced Griever 183
The Scarf 183
Every Day's Damocles 184
Never 185
For a Woman Grown Cold 185
Of Any Poet 186
Tract on Living 187
Maker of Songs 190
For a Lost Grave 191
Interim 192
Cooling Song 193
Noon 194
Night 195
They Say Her Heart Is Broken 196
Said to a Bird 197
Submergence 197
Woman Death 198
Words for Weeping 200
Breath 201
A Woman Ponders 202
The Tired Mortal 203
Estranged 204

Any Woman 205
Broken Moon 206
The Unuttered 207
The Silent Bard 208
The Relinquisher 209
Death Defied 210
The Lost Hill 210
Crossed Heart 211
Song to Be Known Before Death 212
Flight 213
Sleep Charm 213
Riddle 214
Slow Death 215
Protest 216
Hearsay 217

Notes and Bibliography 218
Index of Titles 223
Index of First Lines 225

Introduction

Over and under,
Under and out.
Thread that is fibre,
Thread that is stout.

I'm not singing;
I'm sewing ...
  ("*Stitches*")

We enter a poem by Hazel Hall through a narrow space, often
the space of the room in which she was confined, which opens
outward into a vivid, often oceanic space, only to return again:

I was sewing a seam one day—
Just this way—
Flashing four silver stitches there
With thread, like this, fine as a hair,
And then four here, and there again,
When
The seam I sewed dropped out of sight...
I saw the sea come rustling in,
Big and grey, windy and bright...
Then my thread that was as thin
As hair, tangled up like smoke
And broke.
I threaded up my needle, then—
Four here, four there, and here again.
  ("*Seams*")

Hall's poems seem on their surfaces tidy, sometimes as strictly
and gorgeously embellished as her needlework. Yet close under
their surfaces we sense the seething of a restless intelligence.
Beginning with the materials at hand—her limited mobility, her
isolation and loneliness, her gifts with needlework and words,
and her exquisite grief—Hazel Hall fashioned in the short span

of her career a poetry of startling achievement and durability. Her three books, reprinted here, are filled with deep silences and singing, portents and lamentations, sensual delights, resignation and compassion. Although sometimes dated in their diction, and now and then verging on the sentimental, the poems are more often strikingly modern, gazing on the world and its "glitter of sterility."

"The facts of my sister's life were few," wrote Ruth Hall.[1] Were it not for the discreet and eloquent letters that Ruth supplied to curious editors and critics, we might know very little about Hazel Hall. Moreover, as Ruth explained, "since my sister was fond of silence and its larger meanings, she heartily disliked discussions of herself as an individual. Rather she would want her poetry to speak of herself."[2]

A few facts are known. Hazel Hall was born in St. Paul, Minnesota, on February 7, 1886, and moved to the bustling young city of Portland, Oregon, as a small child. She had two sisters, Ruth and Lulie. An exuberant, unusually sensitive and imaginative child, she would have experienced keenly the nearby ocean and the dense forests that are such commanding presences in the lives of Northwesterners. But at the age of twelve, following a bout of scarlet fever, possibly complicated by a fall, she was confined to a wheelchair. She lived out her life in an upper room of the family's house on 52 Lucretia Place, overlooking the sidewalk and its passersby, able to smell the ocean on the breeze through her window, seeing the top of a fir tree over an adjacent building, watching birds pass, and the changes of light, the passing seasons. To better observe the world outside, she positioned a small mirror on the sill.

A visitor described her eyes as "large and dark. She seldom smiled–though she was not sad. Her forehead was very broad and full.... She propelled herself in a wheel chair–an ill body confining her within the four walls of her home."[3] Because she was unable to attend school, Hall's formal education ended in the fifth grade. But she continued to read widely, though not "to excess," writes Ruth. "Her own mind was able to furnish her with a kind of instinctive wisdom."[4] She was interested in philosophy and was known to be slowly reading through a history of the field.

To help with family finances, Hall took in sewing. She acquired skill in needlework, and gainfully occupied herself embroidering the sumptuous fabrics of bridal gowns, baby dresses, altar cloths, lingerie, and Bishop's cuffs that figure so lushly in her poems. But early in her twenties, taxed by the strain of needlework, her eyesight began to fail, and she turned to writing poems. The first of these, "To an English Sparrow," appeared in the Boston *Transcript* in 1916, when she was thirty years old, with only eight more years to live. "Her writing-day," reports Ruth, "began usually about noon and lasted until quite late at night…. A very sure line of poetry would flash into her mind, and with this as a nucleus she reared a poem."[5]

Other publications followed, in *Harper's*, *The Century*, *The Bookman*, *Yale Review*, and *New Republic*. In 1920, her poem "Three Girls" was selected as one of the best poems of the year, and she won first prize for poems published in *Contemporary Verse*. Her first book, *Curtains*, appeared in 1921. In that year the *Anthology of Magazine Verse* included nineteen of her poems. A group of her needlework poems received the "Young Poet's Prize" from *Poetry*, and she continued to enjoy the favor of its editor, Harriet Monroe. *Walkers* soon followed, in 1923. In the anthology *Best Poems of the Year*, her work began to reach an audience in England. *Cry of Time*, her last book, assembled by her sister Ruth, appeared posthumously in 1928.

Despite her growing recognition in the early 1920s, Hazel Hall's isolation and privacy remained undisturbed. Her correspondence with editors and other writers was tentative. She hoped for a visit from Vachel Lindsay, a writer whom she admired, and was bitterly disappointed when it did not occur. She avidly read in the journals the poems of her contemporaries, as well as current literary criticism. Edna St. Vincent Millay and Elinor Wylie were among her favorite poets, along with Emily Dickinson, Robert Frost, and Edwin Arlington Robinson. Yet her own writing is not haunted by these poets, and influence on Hazel Hall is not easy to discern. Certainly the Georgian poetics of a writer such as Sara Teasdale, a perfumed and pictorial verse in hymnbook metrics, absent of irony, could speak little of the hardships of Hall's life. Nor would she pretend to the worldliness and sophistication of

Millay and Wylie and the emancipated women of the twenties, though her poems are at times more frankly sensual than theirs.[6] Finally, we sense in her work more of the autumnal clarity of Robert Frost, and the fierce ambivalence, synesthesia, and transcendental longing of Emily Dickinson.

Hall's strategy for escaping her confinement is nowhere more evident than in her first book, *Curtains*. We are invited into a darkened, turbulent room, a place of "eternal winter," the outside world of sun, sky, and footsteps all ghostly, echoes and flickering shadows on the sill and walls. Shut in "where rooms are prison places,"[7] she addresses poems to the door, the floor, window, and stairway. She addresses her feet, unable to transport her. "Of all my room," she laments, "the floor alone / Is not mine." Finally, in "Things That Grow," she recognizes that she must be rooted somewhere in the world in order to exfoliate and awaken "the shining interest of the sky."

Her longed-for roots, and paradoxical means of escape, are into the fertile ground of language, and "fancy," the transforming activity of the liberated imagination. "Counterpanes," her first needlework poem, announces this breakthrough: "I will make myself new thought." Her counterpane is assembled from poem-patches, her "quilt of many hues" that will protect her from the "smothered whine/ Of four grey walls' grey wind." Hall finds in the enforced silence a creative source and solace, obliterating "vague realities," and uncertainties. "Now at last with glamour gone," she says, "I can see the naked dawn." Though skepticism and despair continue to darken and threaten her vision, her course is set.

As both seamstress and poet, Hall enjoyed the fortuitous coincidence of two activities that continuously, ingeniously, referred to and informed each other, an interplay of song and stitch. In the needlework poems, Hall's life and her art effortlessly converge, resulting in breathtaking sorties beyond her window, into the world of our shared experience. "Knitting Needles," the first of this sequence, chronicles the recognition of a calling, as the author sorts through her great-grandmother's "trunkful of remembering things,"

But the most remembering of all are her knitting needles.
They are made of black bone
And gleam with sudden creamy light, like lacquer.
When I touch them
They are cold with the death of many years.
Then quickly they take on a sensuous warmth,
And speak under my knitting hands.

Sewing in this ghostly company, Hall identifies in her great-grandmother a muse who instructs her to stitch and speak, releasing her briefly from the confines of her room. Through the ritual of sewing, Hall recovers the memories and vivid sensations of her childhood. Her sensuality is rediscovered, and with it a sexual insistence presses up through poems such as "Lingerie" and "Filet Crochet," a possibility that is reluctantly denied, her needle "strangling tight, / Choking out anything that might" climb the trellis to her window. Through needlework, however, Hall was able to transform her loss into something of value, utility, and beauty. Having sewn (and written) all day, she would have by tomorrow, "something sorrow has made."

The needlework poems are metrically freer in form than the work preceding or following them. Ellipses and dashes, reminiscent of Dickinson's, proliferate. We sense that the urgency and originality of these poems will not be confined within her usual prosodic constraints. And the imagery is more daring:

My hands are motion; they cannot rest.
They are the foam upon the sea...
("Sewing Hands")

Startling for their range and reach, the sewing poems become at times oracular, foreseeing the eventual death of the bride for whom she sews in "Monograms," and even the baby in "A Baby's Dress." In "Late Hours," she sees the fate of the passersby, "I know each pulsing tread / Is spinning out a life's fine thread."

In "Bead Work," Hall creates a facsimile of her lost world, picking up beads like "lobes of light," choosing the color and form of wood and leaves. Elsewhere, she breathes life into the cross-stitched macaws, which are "alert and listening." In "Habit," the poet gazes from her window at the night sky and begins reflexively to "feather-stitch a ring around the moon." And the world reciprocates in "Heavy Threads," stitching *her*, at dawn the "hours of light / ... about to thrust themselves into me / Like omnivorous needles into listless cloth." The myth of Arachne, which is likely to have been familiar to Hazel Hall, suggests itself here. A simple girl, Arachne had the gift for weaving tapestries so lifelike that the forms seemed to breathe and move. Like a goddess, she had the power to create the world. But so great was her hubris that she challenged Athene, goddess of spinning, weaving, and needlework, to a contest of their skills. Enraged not only by Arachne's audacity, but also by her accomplishment, and not wishing to destroy such a gift, Athene changed the girl into a spider. Hall's frequent comparison of the thread of her stitches to her own hair suggests that, like Arachne, she is sewing out of herself. The poet as spider, her web ruined by death, will appear later in the poem "Intelligence" from *Cry of Time*.

Beginning with artifacts and stories of her grandmother and her great-grandmother, Hall's memory grows ever more inclusive, coming to involve all working and sorrowing women, sewing together in concert:

> Other hands are teaching
> My needle; when I sew
> I feel the cool, thin fingers
> Of hands I do not know.
>
> . . .
>
> All the tired women,
> Who sewed their lives away,
> Speak in my deft fingers
> As I sew to-day.
>
> (*"Instruction"*)

In poems like "Defeat" and, especially, "Late Sewing," the final poem in the needlework sequence, gorgeous descending figures recapitulate Hall's despairing sense of the futility of artistic creation, and its presumption. Perhaps mindful of Arachne's fate, Hall describes her singing and sewing as "a little travesty on life," a work so flawed and inadequate that it manages only a grotesque imitation of reality. The dark bouquet of April poems that concludes *Curtains* reiterates her foreboding that her art will be found insufficient, that the "counterpane" of her poems will finally be torn away by the smothering grey wind. In these final poems, April "chokes me with fragrance" and closes "like a hand around my throat." Hazel Hall's confrontation with death will be played out in the *danse macabre* of her last book, *Cry of Time*.

The subject of needlework that illuminates *Curtains* will not, except for occasional mention, be returned to again. When Hall stopped sewing–her eyesight failing–she appears to have stopped writing about sewing and turned her attention outward to the mysterious otherness of the walkers passing beneath her window. Where *Curtains* was a private, and interior book, *Walkers* is populated, at times even crowded. The pedestrians, each singular, each given an individual poem, are sometimes real, yet at other times seem ghostly figments or projections. In "A Boy Went By," the child is present in the flesh, "inimitable" and "inviolate." But the old woman who follows in the next poem is clothed in "stricken sound / And shadow" like a shroud.

Walkers is a book of longing, and reaching out, for human fellowship. In *Curtains*, Hall worked through, and grew weary of, the possibilities for transcendence and transformation, exhausting, in "After Embroidering," even the sewing trope. She could work into cloth a clever imitation of a landscape:

> But if I go farther,
> If I follow the path,
> Fling out the gate,
> Plunge one breathless thought over an horizon...
> My hands lose their cunning.

In *Walkers*, in poems such as "Three Girls" and "Walking," Hall projects herself imaginatively through her window, vicariously walking and communing with others. She creates for each a sly variation on the walker's andante music, tripping iambs for the young, shuffling dactyls for the old, hesitations, meanderings, or stridings forward, "motion, and [in her poem] echoed motion."

Time blows like an eroding wind over and through the lives of the walkers, and through the poems–everything is fleeting, passing, dying. A powerful long sequence at the heart of this book, "Footfalls," reads like the poet's requiem for herself, and a triumphal summation of her life and wisdom. "There's a better way / To die," she asserts, "than to die of sorrow."

> And whatever the dying be,
> Companioned by winds that stalk
> Beside us undyingly,
> Let us walk, walk....
>   (*"Footfalls V"*)

The spectral walkers drifting through these poems arouse in Hall a radical modernist uncertainty: do others exist at all for us, and in what way? These same insubstantial others might have stepped from a page of Fernando Pessoa or T.S. Eliot. Masks and self-deception, identity and the danger of losing it, become central concerns: we "strive to find and struggle to hold / The meaning of [our] own identity." The poems are darkened by portents, dangers, and warnings, our fates "whirring" around us like dust on the street. Hall saw the human condition as yoked and dumb, linking us to each other and to death, and this knowledge "weighs unbearably" on her. Children, especially, in poems such as "A Child On the Street" and "At the Corner," are pursued by "relentless destinies." The footfalls of the walkers become a dark drumbeat, a death march: "the truth your feet speak to the ground."

Hazel Hall's compassion extended even to walkers as yet unborn. In "They Will Come," "the sound of their tread is a cry / Moving along my mind," and she sorrows proleptically for them:

> All that others have known of longing and pain
> Will be immeasurably theirs; they must reckon and face
> Rapture unknown, then pass like the rain
> Drifting on into space.

A deep uneasiness weighs on the final poems in *Walkers*. In "Today," Hall turns away, and denies the passersby, "tired of the bells in their feet / Ringing ceaselessly." Like Emily Dickinson, she recoils from the trite ("Prayer Against Triteness"), and longs to sing "what was never heard." At last she seems to welcome, almost to beckon, death, "the green and useful grave." "I will feel nothing," she says, and coolly celebrates the apocalypse, that "incomparable incident." Although *Walkers* ends with a reprisal of the theme of transcendental longing, the inevitability of death has been accepted.

Cry of Time is a book of lamentations, and a book of farewells. A new severity and intensity surges through these last poems, propelled by a more muscular diction: the light is "baffled," the dark like "twisted iron," the night "chronic." The outer world has grown strange, an unreal place of time and death, where the sunlight is sword-like, steely, cold and rigid, the moonlight "like ice… hard and sheer." Through her window, Hall sees twisted steel and brittle glass, the hills folded like pieces of paper. But her interior world, her refuge, is ever-curved and curving: the contour of her hand and cheek, the curve of breath, the curving arc of thought, the "quiet curve of sorrow." A darkly mellifluous lyricism celebrates this inner life. In *Cry of Time*, Hall once again finds in silence a creative source; her song is a "silence that is heard," her "cry of time" the cry of human mortality.

Shadowing Hall's hard-won success is a deepening dissatisfaction with poetry and a keen awareness of its inadequacies. Weary of her craft, she casts a critical eye back over her poems, perhaps noticing the occasional preciousness in *Curtains* and the portentousness in *Walkers*. In numerous poems, the reader, Hall's "audience," addresses the poet, usually to criticize. While she at least once invokes her muse, Hall's final poems turn more often against poetry. "Think of me listening myself to death," from "Pleasantry," recalls Adrienne Rich's, "what kind of beast would turn its life into words?"[8] Shedding her past, Hall places a moratorium on sorrow, and even on the sea, her previous emblem of irrepressible life, going metaphorically "inland" to "soundlessness." She would even, in

"To All Quiet Persons," shed wisdom in favor of experience, however mortal: "come out into the sunlight, come."

Blindness and physical decline are recurring themes in *Cry of Time*. "For a Broken Needle" reads as a dual elegy for the needle and the poet of the needlework poems:

FOR A BROKEN NEEDLE
Even fine steel thinly made
To hold a raging thread,
Comes to lie with purple shade
In a dreaded bed.

All its chiseled length, its nice
Grip, its moving gleam
That was once like chips of ice
In a heated seam,

Are no more. It is fit
We should chant a strain
Of lament, then tumble it
Out into the rain.

In this poem, as well as others ("Weeper in the Dark," "The Dubious Self," and "Rain"), Hall draws near to death, finding there release and comfort, losing herself, dissolving, merging, or vanishing. The life-giving ocean now crashes over her, and she is insensible as a stone. Even the erotic and sensual are drawn into the vortex of death. Hall walks in these poems "close to the blinding edge / Of night." A new elegiac tone floods the writing, a tone of resignation and acceptance, finding that "cold is easier than pain."

Cry of Time is punctuated by poems describing an indivisible solidarity between women, a sisterhood of which Hazel Hall felt a part. This theme, introduced in *Curtains*, and visited in *Walkers*, we find brilliantly elaborated here, in poems such as "Inheritance," "Woman Death," and "Any Woman." Here women's solitude and grief is described collectively. In these poems, more than in any of her others, Hall touches—indeed embraces—others, experiencing the discharge of empathy she so longed for.

Dubious of poetry, her health failing, Hall affirmed at the end the endurance of *song*. Sewing and singing merge a last time in "Maker of Songs," where the speaker instructs herself to

> Take strands of speech, faded and broken;
> Tear them to pieces, word from word,
> Then take the ravelled shreds and dye them
> With meanings that were never heard.
>
> . . .
>
> . . . Weaver,
> Weave well and not with words alone;
> Weave through the pattern every fragment
> Of glittered breath that you have known.

Song will survive, if only as dirge, "a riot / Of silences... a quiet / That yet may snare the flesh." The interior landscape of *Cry of Time* is crisscrossed by a bird, image of freedom, its thin wing curving, "crushing space / With the arrow of its breast."

The poet *in extremis*, a poem such as "They Say Her Heart Is Broken," releases brilliant spasms of modernist invention, nervously indexing a shattered reality, resembling uncannily the poems of Sylvia Plath. In "Estranged" ("I have broken with myself"), the voice seems disembodied. In "The Unuttered," Hall achieves a dense distillation of loss, a mingling of grief and physical pain, making, paradoxically, a "good love." And in "The Relinquisher" she rids even her blood of the sound of the sea. As if bequeathing her life's accumulated possessions to the reader, she reaches the end of her list, her hands, in *Curtains* so empowering, now "the exquisite frail mirrors / Of all the mind misunderstands."

In these poems, many of which were written in the final weeks of her life, Hazel Hall makes her peace with her art, with her world, even, in "Interim," with sorrow itself:

> Let us have nothing more to say of sorrow.
> Our world's concern is but a twisted leaf
> Blown down the shadowed verities of grief,
> Falling into the silence whence it came.

She comes to quietus, approaching the edge, where time is "purple." She leaves the reader in an empty room, filled with quietly reverberating interrogations.

> What my fingers had of shape
> Is a curve of blowing light,
> Moving in unhurried flight,
> With the rain, to its escape.
>
> Yet what have I given rain,
> Who have felt the edge of rain
> Fray my fingers, who have striven
> To give much, what have I given
> But a little moving pain?
>
> ("Rain")

The critical response to Hazel Hall's poems appears to have been immediate and enthusiastic. William Stanley Braithwaite rhapsodized in the Boston *Transcript*, "Out of the West comes a woman poet to dispute the sovereignty of Sara Teasdale."[9] The more demure *Poetry* magazine said of *Curtains*, "The usual first book of verse is conglomerate…. But this is the crystallization of a personality."[10] And the reviewer of *Cry of Time* for the New York *World* wrote:

> This poetry is so tenuously delicate that only its cumulative power could have made the world note it. There are things in it as subtle and sudden as Emily Dickinson, and things as accurate, sharp and metallic as E.E. Cummings; but Hazel Hall was so far from being derivative that her poems are stamped with an almost fiercely individual impress.[11]

The publication of each of Hazel Hall's books caused an excited stir in the nation's literary community. Yet by the mid-1930s she had been largely forgotten, and her poems had vanished from the anthologies. We can only speculate why her star, having risen so quickly, should have suddenly dimmed. It is true that Hall lacked the supporting circle of friends and literary connections that often propel a career. It must be admitted that her second book, Walkers, is less even in quality than Curtains or Cry of Time. And it is certainly possible that Hall was mistakenly identified in the minds of many with the domestic, and forgettable, "women poets" who wrote sentimental verse on subjects such as sewing. Or did some at the time find it difficult to approach Hall's ferociously grieving and inconsolable spirit, her "raging thread" and "chronic night," the very qualities that make her poems so alive and compelling today?

After a long eclipse, Hazel Hall's poems have been rediscovered, and are once again being read and celebrated. The volume in hand gathers for the first time all her poetry published in book form. It restores to *Walkers* two poems, "Ahead of Him" and "A Whistler in the Night," listed in the contents, but unaccountably absent from some copies of the book. Not included here are the numerous unpublished works; the poems published pseudonymously (some twenty poems under one pseudonym alone), mostly juvenilia in which the poet was still finding her identity and voice; and her attempts at short prose, of which three are known to have been published.[12] The reader will find here *Curtains*, *Walkers*, and *Cry of Time* in their entirety, making possible a complete appreciation of Hazel Hall's achievement, and a reassessment of her place among American poets. Ahead of their time, perhaps these poems have had to await a new generation of readers, the unborn walkers for whom she sang.

John Witte
Eugene, Oregon
August 1999

CURTAINS

I have curtained my window with filmy seeming,
Overhanging it with chintz of dreaming,
That I may watch through sun and rain
Beside the windowpane.

Faintly my curtains stir and flutter
Before the words that loud rains utter,
And through their fabric, cool and still,
The sun falls on the sill.

Part One
CURTAINS

Frames

Brown window-sill, you hold my all of skies,
And all I know of springing year and fall,
And everything of earth that greets my eyes—
Brown window-sill, how can you hold it all?

Grey walls, my days are bound within your hold,
Cast there and lost like pebbles in a sea;
And all my thought is squared to fit your mould—
Grey wall, how mighty is your masonry!

June Night

Into my room to-night came June,
A band of stars caught up her hair,
And woven of the mist of moon,
And patterned from the leaf-laced air,
Her garments spread a soft perfume
Over the shadows of my room.

But hardly had her coming stirred
My darkness with a hope like dawn,
Or had my anxious silence heard
Her faint footfall, than she was gone.
She went as though with a quick fear
Of the eternal winter here.

Sun Glamour

The day has brought me sun-loaned cheer,
And to unchangeable ways, change...
But dusk is here to make them strange,
Making them clear.

THE WORLD'S VOICE

If I listen shall I hear
Sounds that seem to hover near?
Speech of ship calling to ship
Through dark tides that twist and grip,
Dash of spray on a splintered coast,
The whisper-flutter of a host
Of sun-coloured butterflies
Wheeling under marbled skies;
The jabber of a little wind
Where the meadows' grass is thinned–
Or where trees forget their prides
To sway in unison like tides;
All the city's formal din;
All the hush where big streets thin
To little crooked lanes and lose
Themselves as the green distance blues
Into space–Oh everything
That can either sound or sing!

To-day my four grey walls are strung
So thin, each echo has a tongue;
The world has raised its voice to-day
That I may hear what it has to say.

I listen...
        What I hear
Is only the longing of an ear
Too much concerned with the cry of space,
And with listening in a quiet place.

SEASONS

Winter, spring, summer and fall–
Shadow-lights upon a wall:

Gleams of grey fleeing the path
Where the wind walks cold with wrath;

Yellow-fluttered petalled things
Like flower ghosts of other springs;

Curtains of dull, sticky gold,
Smothering hours in their fold;

Smoky rays that stir and creep
Aimlessly, like tired sheep.

Winter, spring, summer and fall–
Shadows fading on a wall.

FOOTSTEPS

They pass so close, the people on the street;
Footfall, footfall;
I know them from their footsteps' pulsing beat;
Footfall, footfall;
The tripping, lingering and the heavy feet;
I hear them call:

I am the dance of youth, and life is fair!
Footfall, footfall;
I am a dream, divinely unaware!
Footfall, footfall;
I am the burden of an old despair!
Footfall...

To a Door

Door, you stand in your darkened frame
Mindful of your wooden might,
Flaunting relentlessly your claim
As guardian of sound and light.

Yet for all your vigil, Door,
Shadows that slip on panting feet
Over your threshold tinge the floor
With what was sunlight on the street.

And sounds fluttering in to die
(Door, you thought I should not know!)
Were started by an echo's cry
That was a voice not long ago.

Floor of a Room

The walls and windows of my room,
With stolid constancy
Spreading checkered light or gloom,
Belong to me.
Of all my room the floor alone
Is not my own.

Days, like armfuls of fresh flowers
Slowly… I scatter there;
Yet for my offering of hours
I may share
Only the cold, disquiet rest
Of a passing guest.

Always I must waive my rights
To feet, who, strange and still,
Press their claims on windy nights;
And not until
I come again, another ghost,
Shall I be host.

THE HAND-GLASS

I am holding up a mirror
To look at life; in my hand-glass
I see a strange, hushed street below me
Where people pass.
The street is coloured like a picture,
And people passing there
Move with the majesty of story,
And are less real and wise than fair.

Looking at life in a mirror
Is distortion. I must see
Through the paint the flimsy canvas,
I must be
Cynical, and judge no passer
By the colour of a dress—
O eyes that must learn from a mirror,
Search for dust and bitterness!

SILENCE

Silence is the sound of footsteps
Hushed upon a stair,
The fluttering of ruffled garments,
A song's forgotten air–
All the old, forbidden echoes
That quenched their fevers there.

Things That Grow

I like the things with roots that know the earth,
Trees whose feet, nimble and brown,
Wander around in the house of their birth
Until they learn, by growing down,
To build with branches in the air;
Ivy-vines that have known the loam
And over trellis and rustic stair,
Or old grey houses, love to roam;
And flowers pushing vehement heads,
Like flames from a fire's hidden glow,
Through the seething soil in garden-beds.
Yet I, who am forbidden to know
The feel of earth, once thought to make
Singing out of a heart's old cry!
Untaught by earth how could I wake
The shining interest of the sky?

STAIRWAYS

Why do I think of stairways
With a rush of hurt surprise?
Wistful as forgotten love
In remembered eyes;
And fitful as the flutter
Of little draughts of air
That linger on a stairway
As though they loved it there.

New and shining stairways,
Stairways worn and old,
Where rooms are prison places
And corridors are cold,
You intrigue with fancy,
You challenge with a lore
Elusive as a moon's light
Shadowing a floor.

You speak to me not only
With the lure of storied art–
For wonder of old footsteps
Lies lightly on my heart;
And more than the reminiscence
Of yesterday's renown–
Laughter that might have floated up,
Echoes that should drift down.

Night Silence

A great mouth, lean and grey,
Munching the sounds of day:
Last voices and the beat
Of weather and late feet.

Gently parted lips
Telling of high white ships
That sail the imaged seas
Of borrowed memories.

Inexorable lips shut tight
Over the tongue of the night...

Suddenly the sick sound
Of crickets on the ground,
Or the long shuddering bark
Of a dog into the dark...

Insinuations of vain
Forgetfulness of pain,
Taunts of old moonlights
And other sound-stung nights.

COUNTERPANES

I will make myself new thought;
My own is worn and old.
And old counterpanes will not
Keep out the wind and cold.

From borrowed thought I will choose
Pieces, and, row on row,
Patch a quilt of many hues
Like the quilts of long ago.

It cannot be so fine
As what the years have thinned,
But I dread the smothered whine
Of four grey walls' grey wind.

I will patch me a counterpane,
For mine is worn to scars,
And I fear the iron rain
Of a ceiling's splashing stars.

PASSERS-BY

You–and you, Passer-by–and you;
You, languid feet, and you, wild to climb,
Seeking your respite or star-rimmed view,
Where do you go down the streets of Time?

Never the same, yet ever the same–
You and you, hurrying, slow,
Crowding the way with your motley claim
Of life, always you come and go.

You, stung with purpose. You, driven by
Blindly before Creation's sweep.
Are there ways for the searchers of stars on high?
And other ways for the seekers of sleep?

Or only one way for all to run?...
Only one sound drifts up to me,
The blend of every tread in one,
Impersonal as the beat of the sea.

LATE WINTER

I am content with latticed sights:
A lean grey bough, a frill
Of filmy cloud, the shadow-lights
Upon a window-sill.

I am content in wintered days
With all my eyes may meet.
April, when you dance down these ways
Hush your awakening feet.

BECAUSE OF JONQUILS

A ray of jonquils thrills the grey
And frowning winter of a room...
Out from the depths of an old day
A burst of spring-light cuts its way,
Lifting the vague perfume
Of walled-in gardens long, long dumb,
Of blooms that never bloomed at all...
Then quickly, as autumn's keen winds come,
Shadows, like dead leaves, fall.

Unseen

Often I am awaked from sleep to see—
Framed like a picture by the dark of night—
The sweep of space above a frozen height,
Or, lifting from a skyline, one dead tree.
Again it is the full tide leaping free
Over black rocks, or breaking blue and white.
Again, a rill that in leaf-filtered light,
With words of rustling water, calls to me.

These are not dreams of beauty I have known,
Nor mine the interest remembrance brings;
Only my fancy knows the tides' deep tone,
Only my longing seeks the tangled springs...
And yet they make a clearer, wilder call
Than if a fond remembering were all.

COMPANY

A footstep sounded from the street...
Listening, I knew of you!
With the good singing of your feet
You came in, too.

Companioned by the sun and rain,
Mingling with the winds at will,
You passed, but in your step's refrain
I have you still.

A CHILD DANCING

A child with unmanageable feet
Skips on the street below;
The wind has invited her to race,
The sun is a kiss upon her face
And the world a great applauding place.
I know...

She dances now with timid step,
Light as new leaves blow.
Her skirts are wings of butterflies,
And with every feathery grace she tries
Her feet cry out life's glad surprise...
I know...

ROADS

One road leads out to the country-side;
One road goes by on its way to town;
And always, as long as the sun is guide,
The feet that love them go up and down.

After the evening star's white light
Has lured from the hills or the lighted town,
There are other feet all through the night,
Following dreams up and down.

THE ROOM UPSTAIRS

Room just above me
Over my own,
I have not seen you,
I have not known
Where your big bed stands,
Where is your chair,
Whether your windows
Look here or look there.

Room just above me,
Long have I kept
Vigil below you
While others slept,
Thinking of the footsteps
Known to your floor,
Which passed from your threshold
To come there no more.

Room just above me,
To-night it seems
There is new creaking
Over your beams;
It might be the night-wind,
It might be the tread
Of one who is lonely,
Or bored, being dead.

THE PROUD STEED

I plunge at the rearing hours;
Life is a steed of pride,
Who so high above me towers
I cannot mount and ride.

SONGS FOR DREAMS

Some dreams that I have loved
And dreamed by night and day,
Though they are lost to me,
Are never far away.

A part of lurking winds,
Of silence in grey rooms—
From every echoed sound,
And out of corner-glooms

They come as strange as ghosts,
A little death-sad throng,
Beseeching me with praying hands
To give them life in song.

Nobody Passes

Nobody passes on the street.
The day is set, like a stage, for feet,
With a ridge of white clouds painted high
Across the canvas of the sky;
With pavement gleaming and too clean;
A shimmer of grass that seems too green,
And houses alert on every side
Showing a stiff and conscious pride.
The day is a stage, and life is a play–
But nobody passes down this way.

SHADOWS

One shadow on my wall, an intimate
Of dusk, comes only when it comes alone.
It lifts out of new dark and spreads a great
Wing of quiet where once the sun has shone,
Cooling the air like rain on stone.

Such shadow might find entrance to a tomb,
And be at home in places where the dead
Are fitful sleepers; moving through gloom
It might lay benediction on a head
That death has left uncomforted.

Twilight

Tiptoeing twilight,
Before you pass,
Bathe light my spirit
As dew bathes grass.

Quiet the longing
Of my hands that yearn,
As you fold the flower
And hush the fern.

Guard me with shadows
To fortify
My failing purpose,
My tired eye,

That in your stillness
I may relight
My faith's frail candle
Before the night.

ECSTASY

For moments of this life's swift cycle made
Commemorable with you, O Ecstasy,
Shall we be reconciled in worlds to be,
Shall we find recompense when death is paid?
I can imagine in eternal shade
Solace for tired dreams, and in the sea
Equivalent for moods of stress or glee;
In stars an old unrest merged and allayed.

What element can give us, in your name,
Redress which is appreciable before
The concept of the universal mind?
You, who are multiform, to one a flame,
Soul-scourging; to another are defined
In sudden earth-breaths through an opened door.

Captive

My spirit is a captive bird
That beats against its cage all day,
Until its winging strength is whirred
Vainly away.

My spirit learns its impotence
Only when night has blurred its bars.
Wings seem a strange impertinence
Before the stars.

COWARDICE

Discomfort sweeps my quiet as a wind
Leaps at trees and leaves them cold and thinned.
Not that I fear again the mastery
Of winds, for holding my indifference dear
I do not feel illusions stripped from me.
And yet this is a fear—
A fear of old discarded fears, of days
That cried out at irrevocable ways.
I cower for my own old cowardice,
For hours that beat upon the wind's broad breast
With hands as impotent as leaves are; this
Robs my new hour of rest.

I thought my pride had covered long ago
All the old scars, like broken twigs in snow.
I thought to luxuriate in rich decay,
As some far-seeing tree upon a hill;
But startled into shame for an old day
I find that I am but a coward still.

Before Thought

Dawn paints quaint histories
In pageant on my wall;
Imminent destinies
Concern it not at all.

Shadow-Bound

You whom the shadows beckoned
Long and long ago,
Who taught me the flaming utterance
Of words, now strange and slow
On my lips that loved them
Long–Oh, long ago…

Why have you stirred the silence
That flowered from my pain?
Just now your anxious footstep
Sounded above the rain;
Just now your eyes, beseeching,
Shadowed my windowpane.

A Falling Star

I hope I shall remember,
The day I come to die,
The welcome of this morning's dawn,
This evening's good-night sky.

I hope I shall remember
The kindly little star,
Caught in to-night's mist-matted hair,
Which greeted me afar.

And how as I was watching,
Loving its little light,
Fleet as a dream it dropped and fell
Into the urn of night.

FEET

Feet, I am weary of your beat;
All day, all year, all life you pass
Below me on the street,
Driven upon my hearing as the grass
Before wild rain and sleet.

You snatch up in your tidal tone
The reaching rhythms of my peace
And substitute your drone,
Until intimidated dreams release
The visions they have known.

Feet, I am weary of your stave—
The little course your sounds pursue—
Weary that I must waive
My reaches in subservience to you,
Who seek only a grave.

FLASH

I am less of myself and more of the sun;
The beat of life is wearing me
To an incomplete oblivion,
Yet not to the certain dignity
Of death. *They cannot even die*
Who have not lived.

               The hungry jaws
Of space snap at my unlearned eye,
And time tears in my flesh like claws.

If I am not life's, if I am not death's,
Out of chaos I must re-reap
The burden of untasted breaths.
Who has not waked may not yet sleep.

ECHOES

Day-long I hear life's sounds beat like the sea;
Day-long, day-long
They sweep their deep tide-rhythms over me,
And as a song
Reiterated, fall unmeaningly.

Where once I bent life's echoes to my will,
Day after day
Following wings of sound over the sill
Far, far away,
Now my sick fancy lies inert and still.

Silence that slowly wraps me with the ease
Of dreamed-out sleep,
Quenches the sound of vague realities
Whose echoes keep
Their rhythms like old winds in drying seas.

LONELINESS

Sometimes when I am long alone
I wonder what is loneliness–
This silence like a deep bell's tone,
These moments, motionless?

This hush above the nervous street?
Removed as is the tree that stands,
Hill-high, with burrowing root-feet
And boughs like reaching hands.

As in my blood I feel life press,
Like sap into the frailest bough,
I think if such is loneliness
Then I am lonely now.

SUNLIGHT THROUGH A WINDOW

Beauty streamed into my hand
In sunlight through a pane of glass;
Now at last I understand
Why suns must pass.

I have held a shadow, cool
Reflection of a burning gold,
And it has been more beautiful
Than hands should hold.

To that delicate tracery
Of light, a force my lips must name
In whispers of uncertainty,
Has answered through me in a flame.

Beauty is a core of fire
To reaching hands; even its far
Passing leaves a hurt desire
Like a scar.

Record

Dreams are eyes fixed on closed doors
And on threshold-lights lighting cold floors.

Dreams are doors swung strangely back
On the wonder of a ribbony track.

Dreams are voices, echoed and thinned,
Calling...drowned out in the wind.

Dreams are feet on the edge of lands
Feeling the suck of hidden sands.

My Song

My song that was a sword is still.
Like a scabbard I have made
A covering with my will
To sheathe its blade.

It had a flashing tongue of steel
That made old shadows start;
It would not let the darkness heal
About my heart.

THE GREY VEIL

Life flings weariness over me
Like a thick grey veil; I see
Through its mesh where suns are cold,
Nights are ancient and dawns are old.

Now at last with glamour gone
I can see the naked dawn;
Gauge the hollow depths of noon,
Coolly question star and moon.

And where fired sunsets pale
I, who wear life's grey veil,
Shall not marvel, shall not care.
No light of earth's however fair,
Robbed of the sting of its surprise,
Can delude my sober eyes.

THE ANSWER

I asked the watchful corners of a ceiling,
And the little darkened cracks the years scrawled there,
Why there are suns, and if there is a purpose
Behind this mask of life that people wear.

I asked some gnarled and patient shadows groping
Like wise hands of old blind men, on my wall;
And everything I asked answered my question
With that one answer which does well for all.

HOURS

I have known hours built like cities,
House on grey house, with streets between
That lead to straggling roads and trail off,
Forgotten in a field of green;

Hours made like mountains lifting
White crests out of the fog and rain,
And woven of forbidden music–
Hours eternal in their pain.

Life is a tapestry of hours
Forever mellowing in tone,
Where all things blend, even the longing
For hours I have never known.

The Circle

Dreams—and an old, old waking,
An unspent vision gone;
Night, clean with silence, breaking,
Into loud dawn.

A wonder that is blurring
The new day's strange demands,
The indomitable stirring
Of folded hands.

Then only the hours' pageant
And the drowsing sound of their creep,
Bringing at last the vagrant
Dreams of new sleep.

Defeat

Is this defeat then, after all—
This new indifference to the street,
This unfelt weight of roof and wall—
Is this defeat?

I thought to make my spirit wear
Glittering garments of unrest,
To keep my keen, knife-edged despair
Unsheathed and brilliantly unrepressed.

But days have worn my unrest thin;
Time's soft fingers gently close
Over my outstretched hand, and in
Their certain touch I feel repose.

This is defeat; I will submit,
Resigned to the quieting decree
Of defeat that is indefinite
As victory.

The Impartial Giver

I who have spent my hands in futile weaving,
And you who flung yours out before the sun,
For all you held, for all my restless grieving,
What have you, more than I have, really won?

My industry has faltered; through your fingers
Your sunlight sifts like finely running sands;
And Time shall bring us, when the last star lingers,
A cross to hold, made of our humbled hands.

SANDS

My days are like sands; colourless,
Each matched to each, unerringly
They drift. The salt bleach of a sea
Has washed them clean and lustreless;
The teeth of rock on ragged strands
Have ground them to an even grey,
And one wind blows them a one way.

But Oh, the slow making of sands.

All is here; forgotten things
Mix with the unforgettable,
Granite blends with tinted shell,
And nothing so stable that it clings
To its stability. Had there
Been more of marble, more of gold,
The sands would hide in their grim hold
Nothing more wise, nothing more fair.

But Oh, the slow making of sands.

Grain on grain of even grey,
Slowly they drift in the one way
Covering the wreck that stands
Against my beach of life. One mast
Cuts at the sky, the hull is fast
In sand—the slow-made sands that pull
With the wind... covering...
And leaving every broken thing
Hushed and coldly beautiful.

PART TWO

NEEDLEWORK

KNITTING NEEDLES

When my great-grandmother died
She left a trunkful of remembering things.
There are carved boxes of sandalwood
Guarding inconsequential trifles of grave
            consequence,
Like scraps of faded ribbon and broken jewellery
And the ash of a pressed rose.
There are fans of ivory,
Pieces of fine, worn lace,
And bundles of yellowed letters.
But most remembering of all are her knitting needles.
They are made of black bone
And gleam with sudden creamy light, like lacquer.
When I touch them
They are cold with the death of many years.
Then quickly they take on a sensuous warmth,
And speak under my knitting hands:

Long ago…
There was a garden steeped in spring,
And in remembering…
A seat in the shade where flowers were—
A seat in the shade—and a riotous blur
Of colour and scent and sun-gold June…
And the warm-armed mists of last night's moon,
Clouding, shrouding everything
With new remembering…
And every heedless second stirred
At a needle's click, and passed unheard,
Keeping, sweeping Time.

Long ago…
There was a window whose shining pane,
Sun-bright or dimmed with rain,
Framed vistas of an empty day
And a winding road winding away
To end like a ravelled thread,
Winding away to coax a tread,
Yet only echoes might it bring,
Echoes, long remembering—
Echoes, vibrant unsilenced sound
That caught up the days in its spirals and wound
The months, the years, around and around,
And hurled them out of the truth of things
Into the heaven of rememberings…
What mattered the minutes slipping past
Under wan hands—unheeded, fast—
Keeping, leaping Time?

Long ago...
There were grey depths in a white-walled room
Of uncomputed gloom.
There was no sound save a click, click, click,
As even and true as a good clock's tick;
And nothing of musical silence was there
To ease the weight of unwaved air.
Outside there was no winter nor spring,
Within there was no remembering—
There was no need of remembering,
Except to cast on the stitches right;
Only the need of a little light
A little longer—nothing at all
Save the clicking moments' rise and fall,
As, proud in their own importance at last,
They clicked and nicked their way... and passed...
Into Time.

STITCHES

Over and under,
Under and out.
Thread that is fibre,
Thread that is stout.

I'm not singing;
I'm sewing.

Days that are futile,
Days that are wise,
Holding the visions
Of dead men's eyes.

I tell you I'm not singing;
If you hear anything
It's my needle.

Days that are prophets
With prophecies
Blunted and tangled
As Eternity's.

I say if you hear anything–

Life-threaded hours;
Purpose that wraps
Fine stitch on fine stitch–
Then ravels…and snaps.

MONOGRAMS

I am monogramming
Seven dozen napkins,
With tablecloths to match,
For a bride.

Ninety-one times my needle shall trace
The leaf-like scrolls that interlace
Each other; up the padded side
Of the monogram my eye shall guide
For ninety-one days where the stitches run;
And every day one more is done.

She is tall and fair,
She will be married
In June....

The linen is fine as satin is fine;
Its shining coolness flaunts design
Of death-white poppies, trailing ferns
Rioting richly from Grecian urns.

Ghost-flowers.
Cold, cold...

All these patterned splendours fade
Before the crest my hands have made;
In the lifeless flax my stitches cry
With life my hands may not put by.

June...
Real flowers,
Moist and warm to touch,
Like flesh...

And by and by with all the rest
Of intimate things in her bridal-chest,
Gentle muslins and secret lace,
Something of mine will have a place;
Caught in these scrolls and filigrees
There will be that which no eye sees,
The bulk of a season's smothered wonder,
My ninety-one days stitched under and under.

They will be decking an altar
With white roses,
And lacing an aisle
With white ribbon....

LATE HOURS

Crowds are passing on the street,
Tuck on tuck and pleat on pleat
Of people hurrying along,
Homeward bound, throng on throng.
Their work is finished, mine undone;
Still my stitches run.

I cannot watch the people go,
Fold on fold and row on row;
But I know each pulsing tread
Is spinning out a life's fine thread;
I know the stars, like needle-gleams,
Are pricking through the sky's wide seams;
And soon the moon must show its face,
Like a pearl button stitched in place.
All the long hours of the day
Are finished now and folded away;
Yet the hem is still undone
Where my stitches run.

MENDING

Here are old things:
Fraying edges,
Ravelling threads;
And here are scraps of new goods,
Needles and thread,
An expectant thimble,
A pair of silver-toothed scissors.

Thimble on a finger,
New thread through an eye;
Needle, do not linger,
Hurry as you ply.
If you ever would be through
Hurry, scurry, fly!

Here are patches,
Felled edges,
Darned threads,
Strengthening old utility,
Pending the coming of the new.

Yes, I have been mending...
But also,
I have been enacting
A little travesty on life.

BEAD WORK

Restless needle, where my beads
Whip with colour, roll like seeds,
Dive, and pick up one and one,
One and one till we are done;
And fasten each one firm and true
Where the pattern tells you to—
One and one, and one and one.

One and one, and one and one—
Flying needles, as you run,
As you pick up the lobes of light
Mind you guide each sparkle right;
Mind this tawny brown you choose,
Shading it with light wood hues,
When you shape the curving rim
Of this great basket, on whose brim
Heap the designated green,
From new-leaf shades to laurel's sheen.
Then with dawn-pinks and heavy reds
Paint the drowsy roses' heads.
Let dreamy mauves and tones of brass,
And bits of blue in mosaic mass,
Speak for the tints of timid bloom
Which share the shadows' checkered gloom...
Sleepy flowers,
Speeding hours,
Hours, flowers, hours...

SEAMS

I was sewing a seam one day—
Just this way—
Flashing four silver stitches there
With thread, like this, fine as a hair,
And then four here, and there again,
When
The seam I sewed dropped out of sight...
I saw the sea come rustling in,
Big and grey, windy and bright...
Then my thread that was as thin
As hair, tangled up like smoke
And broke.
I threaded up my needle, then—
Four here, four there, and here again.

FINISHED TO-NIGHT

I have unleashed my hands, like hounds,
And I must not call them back;
They are off with virile bounds
On the hidden quarry's track.

Though there come rain or sun—
Fleet and lean and white,
They will follow the scent until they run
The quarry to earth, and the quarry is night.

A Baby's Dress

It is made of finest linen—
Sheer as wasp-wings;
It is made with a flowing panel
Down the front,
All overrun with fagot-stitched bow-knots
Holding hours and hours
Of fairy-white forget-me-nots.

And it is finished.
To-night, crisp with new pressing,
It lies stiffly in its pasteboard box,
Smothered in folds of tissue paper
Which envelop it like a shroud—
In its coffin-shaped pasteboard box.

To-morrow a baby will wear it at a christening;
To-morrow the dead-white of its linen
Will glow with the tint of baby skin;
And out of its filmy mystery
There will reach
Baby hands…

But to-night the lamplight plays over it and finds it cold.
Like the flower-husk of a little soul,
Which, new-lived, has fluttered to its destiny,
It lies in its coffin-shaped pasteboard box.

To-morrow will make it what hands cannot:
Limp and warm with babyness,
A hallowed thing,
A baby's dress.

CROSS-STITCH

I put one little slanting stitch
On another little slanting stitch,
Forming rows of crisscross squares,
Until I had made a peacock;
And always my hands tingled
With the song of my needle:

A little crisscross stitch I take—
Yellow and green and blue;
Out of a sea of them I make
Beautiful peacock you.

Yet finished,
He disappointed me,
And I shuddered at his restraint.
But that night
When he walked out of the sleepy shadows,
With one wink of a wicked, yellow-lidded eye,
I was satisfied.

I took a thread of every shade—
Yellow and green and blue;
Out of a sea of them I made
Beautiful peacock you.

PLAIN SEWING

My stitches, like the even tide of feet
Beating against the pavement of the street
Below my window-sill, forever run
Before the footsteps of the sun.

Down streets of seams, and formal avenues
Of basted hems, each crowding stitch pursues,
Seeking no destination on the way–
Only the end of day.

SEWING HANDS

My hands are motion; they cannot rest.
They are the foam upon the sea,
Borne with a wave to a fleeting crest,
Hurled back, borne on, unceasingly.

They are existent and made whole
In their unrest, as the entity
Of foam is spun where waters roll
Back, and on, eternally.

LINGERIE

To-day my hands have been flattered
With the cool-finger touch of thin linen,
And I have unwound
Yards of soft, folded nainsook
From a stiff bolt.
Also I have held a piece of lawn
While it marbled with light
In a sudden quiver of sun.

So to-night I know of the delicate pleasure
Of white-handed women
Who like to touch smooth linen handkerchiefs,
And of the baby's tactual surprise
In closing its fist
Over a handful of nainsook,
And even something of the secret pride of the girl
As the folds of her fine lawn nightgown
Breathe against her body.

FILET CROCHET

I make a band of filet crochet,
And this is the pattern I never forget:
A rose, a wreath and the latticed net
Of fine filet crochet.

Thread over needle, and over again:
Lattice, a wreath and a single rose—
That is the way the pattern goes
Over and over again.

Finish the rose and start the wreath,
And careful lest, O hurrying thread,
Something climbs over the lattice instead
Of a single rose and a wreath.

Finish the wreath and start the rose,
And pull in, needle, strangling tight,
Choking out anything else that might
Climb with a wreath and a rose.

Under, needle; and over, thread;
Something may grow by a garden wall,
Yet nothing must grow in a pattern at all
But a rose and a wreath of thread.

So thread over needle, and over again,
Until there is nothing else that grows—
Only a wreath and a thready rose
Over and over again.

Heavy Threads

When the dawn unfolds like a bolt of ribbon
Thrown through my window,
I know that hours of light
Are about to thrust themselves into me
Like omnivorous needles into listless cloth,
Threaded with the heavy colours of the sun.
They seem altogether too eager
To embroider this thing of mine,
My Day,
Into the strict patterns of an altar cloth;
Or at least to stitch it into a useful garment.
But I know they will do nothing of the kind.
They will prick away,
And when they are through with it
It will look like the patch quilt my grandmother made
When she was learning to sew.

BUTTONHOLES

Cut a little opening
And overcast it, then
(Throwing the thread across each stitch)
Stitch it round again.

A moment's stitching finds it
Finished; but not until
The sun has burned its beauty out
And dropped behind the hill.

PUZZLED STITCHES

Needle, running in and out,
In and out, in and out,
Do you know what you're about,
In and out, in and out?

Fingers, going to and fro,
To and fro, to and fro,
Do you know the path you go?
To and fro, to and fro?

I might tell you why you're taking
Such good stitches: You are making
Out of linen, fine as breaking
Ocean-spray upon a bluff
Pleating for a Bishop's cuff!

I might make you understand
That a Bishop's white, white hand,
Because of you, will be more fair,
Will be raised in better prayer.

Even then would you know
Why you're going to and fro?
Would you doubt what you're about,
Running in and running out?

Summer Sewing

Lengths of lawn and dimities,
Dainty, smooth and cool,
In their possibilities
Beautiful,

Stretch beneath my hand in sheets,
Fragrant from the loom,
Like a field of marguerites
All in bloom.

Where my scissors' footsteps pass
Fluttering furrows break,
As the scythe trails through the grass
Its deep wake.

All my stitches, running fleet,
Cannot match the tread
Of my thoughts whose wingèd feet
Race ahead.

They are gathering imagery
Out of time and space,
That a needle's artistry
May embrace:

Hints of dawn and thin blue sky,
Breaths the breezes bear,
Wispy-waspy things that fly
In warm air.

Bolts of dimity I take,
Muslin smooth and cool;
These my fingers love to make
Beautiful.

HABIT

Last night when my work was done,
And my estranged hands
Were becoming mutually interested
In such forgotten things as pulses,
I looked out of a window
Into a glittering night sky.

And instantly
I began to feather-stitch a ring around the moon.

PATHS

Needle, you make me remember things…
A path through a wood that ran like wine,
A turn, and the bubbling smell that clings
Close as breath to the lips of springs
Where the sun is sprinkled fine.

Needle, you have a path to run
Where never the boughs of trees have met
And never has seeped the rain of the sun;
But long is the way you have just begun…
Needle, you make me forget.

RIPPING

Ripping, snipping,
Slashing, gnashing
Scissors,
Where the hours left light trail,
Where a needle etched a tale,
Catching in its driven thread
A little something of the sun
Like an adventitous shred
Of gold, in duller weaves misspun;
Something of the swallow-wings
That cut the sky in singing rings,
And something of the intimacy
Of trees whose boughs beckoned my eyes,
The things I had not time to see
Out of the day's unsprung surprise;
(And something... something more:
An incommunicable lore
Which left a trace along these seams
Elusive as the flare
Of a new moon's gleams
Dying on a templed stair....)
Rip and snip,
Slash and gash,
Scissors,
Until your fatal way is run,
And every crying stitch undone;
Until your fine, cold teeth have snipped,
Slashed and gashed, clipped and ripped
Up and down my seams of day....

The teeth of time have just that way.

MADE OF CRÊPE DE CHINE

A needle running in white crêpe de chine
Is not the frail servant of utility
It was designed to be;
It is an arrow of silver sunlight
Plunging with a waterfall.

And hands moving in white crêpe de chine
Are not slaves of the precedent
That governs them;
They are the crouching women of a fountain,
Who have sprung from marble into life
To bathe ecstatically
In the brimming basin.

MEASUREMENTS

Stitches running up a seam
Are not like feet beside a stream,
And the thread that swishes after
Is not at all like echoed laughter.
Yet stitches are as quick as feet,
Leaping from a rocky pleat
To seams that slip like marshy ground;
And thread-swish has a hollow sound.

Stitches that have a seam to sew
Must not forget the way they go,
While feet that find the cool earth sweet
Have forgotten they are feet,
And a laugher cares not why
His echoes have a haunted cry.
So stitches running up a seam
Are not like feet beside a stream,
And the thread that swishes after
Is not at all like echoed laughter.

INSTRUCTION

My hands that guide a needle
In their turn are led
Relentlessly and deftly
As a needle leads a thread.

Other hands are teaching
My needle; when I sew
I feel the cool, thin fingers
Of hands I do not know.

They urge my needle onward,
They smooth my seams, until
The worry of my stitches
Smothers in their skill.

All the tired women,
Who sewed their lives away,
Speak in my deft fingers
As I sew to-day.

THEN THE WIND BLEW

The tops of trees rest my eyes,
Especially the tips of old, dark firs
When they rebel against the small manipulations
Of even air currents,
And leap at the sky.

My Needle's Thread

My needle's thread is long and slow;
As a needle goes a thread must go,
And lame and blind a needle is,
Weighed with a mood's profundities.

My needle's thread is long and slack;
A thread must travel a needle's track,
And a needle leads an aimless course
Labouring against the force
Of gathering thought…
A needle's thread will not be taut
When every stitch is made to feel
Pressure upon the needle's steel
Of coldly flowing reality,
Fluent as waters that find the sea.

My needle's thread is long and slack;
A needle is foiled and driven back
To feel, among its threads, the strands
Of life moving through losing hands.

Two Sewing

The wind is sewing with needles of rain.
With shining needles of rain
It stitches into the thin
Cloth of earth. In,
In, in, in.
Oh, the wind has often sewed with me.
One, two, three.

Spring must have fine things
To wear like other springs.
Of silken green the grass must be
Embroidered. *One and two and three.*
Then every crocus must be made
So subtly as to seem afraid
Of lifting colour from the ground;
And after crocuses the round
Heads of tulips, and all the fair
Intricate garb that Spring will wear.
The wind must sew with needles of rain,
With shining needles of rain,
Stitching into the thin
Cloth of earth, in,
In, in, in,
For all the springs of futurity.
One, two, three.

THE LISTENING MACAWS

Many sewing days ago
I cross-stitched on a black satin bag
Two listening macaws.

They were perched on a stiff branch
With every stitch of their green tails,
Their blue wings, yellow breasts and sharply turned heads,
Alert and listening.

Now sometimes on the edge of relaxation
My thought is caught back,
Like gathers along a gathering thread,
To the listening macaws;
And I am amazed at the futile energy
That has kept them,
Alert to the last stitch,
Listening into their black satin night.

THE LONG DAY

I am sewing out my sorrow,
Like a thread, wearing it thin;
It will be old and frayed to-morrow.
Needle, turn out; needle, turn in.

Sorrow's thread is a long thread.
Needle, one stitch; needle, two.
And sorrow's thread is a strong thread,
But I will wear it through.

Then not only will sorrow
Be old and thin and frayed;
But I shall have to-morrow
Something sorrow has made.

INANIMATE

A needle has no memories;
Less than the stir of frozen trees,
Than unheard rain falling on stone,
Are the seams that it has known.

AFTER EMBROIDERING

I can take mercerized cotton
And make a never-flower beautiful
By thinking of tulips growing in window-boxes;
I can work into cloth
A certain hushed softness
From an imagined scrutiny
Of a lily's skin,
And embroider conventional designs the better
For thinking of brick garden paths.

But if I go farther,
If I follow the path,
Fling out the gate,
Plunge one breathless thought over an horizon...
My hands lose their cunning.

THREE SONGS FOR SEWING

I

A fibre of rain on a windowpane
Talked to a stitching thread:
In the heaviest weather I hold together
The weight of a cloud.

To the fibre of rain on a windowpane
The talkative stitch replied:
I hold together with the weight of a feather
The heaviest shroud.

II

My needle says: Don't be young,
Holding visions in your eyes,
Tasting laughter on your tongue.
Be very old and very wise,
And sew a good seam up and down
In white cloth, red cloth, blue and brown.

My needle says: What is youth
But eyes drunken with the sun
Seeing farther than the truth,
Lips that call, hands that shun
The many seams they have to do
In white cloth, red cloth, brown and blue?

III

One by one, one by one,
Stitches of the hours run
Through the fine seams of the day,
Till like a garment it is done
And laid away.

One by one the days go by,
And suns climb up and down the sky;
One by one their seams are run—
As Time's untiring fingers ply
And life is done.

LATE SEWING

There is nothing new in what is said
By either a needle or a thread:
Stitch, says a needle, *Stitch*, says the thread;
Stitch for the living; stitch for the dead;
All seams measure the same.

Garb for the living is light and gay.
While that for the dead is a shrouding grey,
But all things match on a later day
When little worm-stitches in the clay
Finish all seams the same.

PART THREE

SPRING FROM A WINDOW

BLOSSOM-TIME

So long as there is April
My heart is high,
Lifting up its white dreams
To the sky.

As trees hold up their blossoms
In a blowing cloud,
My hands are reaching,
My hands are proud.

All the crumbled splendours
Of autumn, and the cries
Of winds that I remember
Cannot make me wise.

Like the trees of April
Fearless and fair—
My heart swings its censers
Through the golden air.

In April

Now I am Life's victim—
Cruel victor is he
Who lashes me with colour
Until I ache to see.

Who chokes me with fragrance
Of green things in the rain—
Like a hand around my throat
So sudden is the pain.

Life, I am at your mercy;
And though till I am dead
You torture me with April
I will not bow my head!

When There Is April

Who would fear death when there is April?
Like a flame, like a song,
To heal all who have lived with yearning
Year-through, life-long.

When there is April with fulfilment
For longing and for pain,
For every reaching hand that beauty
Has lured in vain.

Who would shrink from the earth when April
With slim rain hands shall reach
Through the doors of dark, and call them
Who love her speech.

FOREBODING

How shall I keep April
When my songs are done–
How can I be silent
And still feel the sun?

I, who dreaded silence,
I, who April-long
Kept my heart from breaking
With the cry of song.

How can I hold sunlight
In my hands, like gold,
And bear the pain of silence
When my songs are old?

WALKERS

They cool their speech upon the tongue,
They sheathe a dagger in the eye,
Yet like the winds they walk among
They cry themselves in passing by.

An utterance older than the tone
Of words that fall as splintered glass,
Speaks in their rhythmic flesh and bone
And cries their fortunes as they pass.

A Boy Went By

He goes whacking a stick
Against a tree or wall,
Giving a stone a kick,
Or aiming at nothing at all.

And with his grin or stare,
The freckles on his nose,
His aimless, intent air,
An inimitable way he goes.

He, though in making, still
Is in himself complete;
An elemental trill
Echoes behind his feet.

Inviolate even after
Ages of dissenting tongues,
He is incarnate laughter
Lifting from Time's deep lungs.

A Very Old Woman

She passes by though long ago
Time drained the life out of her tread;
She died then, yet she does not know
That she is dead.

Her footsteps are indefinite
With sound, and who are dead should pass
Sandaled as the wind when it
Moves through the grass.

Her shadow twitches on the walk,
And who are not of life should run
Shadowless as a lily's stalk
In full day's sun.

Yet these cling to her: stricken sound
And shadow casting ragged stains;
They drag behind her on the ground
Like broken chains.

It is silence mastering her tread,
Darkness, insidious and slow,
Blotting her imprint... but she is dead
And does not know.

DESTINATIONS

People walking up hill
Say with dubious pace:
A road so ruthless cannot
Lead to a pleasant place.

People walking down hill
Speak with certainty:
This neat road must be leading
To an orchard, or the sea.

THREE GIRLS

Three school girls pass this way each day.
Two of them go in the fluttery way
Of girls, with all that girlhood buys;
But one goes with a dream in her eyes.

Two of them have the eyes of girls
Whose hair is learning scorn of curls,
But the eyes of one are like wide doors
Opening out on misted shores.

And they will go as they go today
On to the end of life's short way;
Two will have what living buys,
And one will have the dream in her eyes.

Two will die as many must,
And fitly dust will welcome dust;
But dust has nothing to do with one—
She dies as soon as her dream is done.

On the Street

Often I watch the walkers on the street.
A sea bird does not lift its sinuous wing
To share the grey wind's wide adventuring
With grace more marvelous than moving feet.
Feet young or wise, defiant and discreet,
With an amazing ease balance and swing,
As in each footstep's even echoing
The slow triumph of time is made complete.

And sometimes I forget what time has told,
Hearing beneath the thud of feet a sound
Articulate as the silence of the sea.
I hear the furtive effort on the ground
Of those who strive to find and struggle to hold
The meaning of their own identity.

Youth

Perhaps his feet might choose in their new pride
A tread whose echoes ring more evenly—
But Life, a friendly hound, runs at his side
And will not let him be.

His spirits answer in good comradeship,
Yet he must have a care to face the street
Erect, lest this strange dignity should slip
Like sandals from his feet.

And in this awkward grace of his new gait,
His show of artlessness, becoming wise,
The past and future gravely arbitrate,
And gaily compromise.

So on he goes with sure, uncertain stride,
Holding with valiant grip his dignity—
But Life, a friendly hound, runs at his side
And will not let him be.

DISPUTED TREAD

Where she steps a whir,
Like dust about her feet,
Follows after her
Down the dustless street.

Something struggles there:
The forces that contend
Violently as to where
Her pathway is to end.

Issues, like great hands, grip
And wrestle for her tread;
One would strive to trip,
And one would goad ahead.

Conflicting strengths in her
Grapple to guide her feet,
Raising an unclean whir,
Like dust, upon the street.

WALKERS AT DUSK

The street fills slowly with the thin
Night light, and fluid shadows pass
Over the roofs as dark pours in
Like dusky wine into a glass.

Out of the gloom I watch them come—
Linked by an invisible chain,
Reconciled to the yoke and dumb
After the heat of pride or pain.

Nothing of the concerns of noon
Remains for them, or serves for me,
But portent, like the unrisen moon,
Begins to weight unbearably.

The Way She Walks

She walks with a gravely conscious tread,
As though she carries above her head
A banner whose flaming inscription runs
In charactery dazzling as the sun's.
And little old winds, like little brown elves,
Run at her side and talk to themselves.

If you look deep as she carries it by
You will see the red inscription's cry:
There is earth below, there is sky above,
And life is music and laughter and love.
You will see the winds, like little brown elves,
Wink at each other and talk to themselves.

Masks

You wear your mask,
And I wear mine;
And we are happy,
For we are fine.

And we are fearless
For what we wear
Gives us valor
Making us fair.

And giving us splendor,
Makes us be
Quick with our hands
In charity.

Yet are you ever
Drenched with a doubt
Lest a passing eye
Should find you out?

Or struck with fear,
Keen as a cry,
That the only deluded
Are you and I?

A CHILD ON THE STREET

Strange that she can keep with ease
A pace so free and fleet,
When such relentless destinies
Stalk at her feet.

Strange she does not see the blur
Where their shadows run
With her footfall, sinister
In the sun.

Some are vague as shadow cast
By clouds where long hills dip,
And some sharp like the broken mast
Of a drifted ship.

Still with her incredulous tread
Defying the darkened ground,
She keeps a pace whose echoes shed
Laughing sound.

And still close at her tripping heel
The old shadows stir,
Deepening as they steal
Nearer her.

A LATE PASSER

Sleep came like rose petals falling on my pillow,
And then a wind of feet
Blew over me, whirling the petals of my slumber
Before it down the street.

SHAWLED

She wraps herself within herself,
Closely, as in a shawl,
And then she hurries down the street
And none of all
The people there who pass her by—
Spending themselves as they go
With a drifting scarf, a brilliant coat—
Can tell what lies below
The heavy folds of her reserve.
Not one will know though she
But covers a thinning garment lest
Their eyes should see;
Or whether she hides a flaming gown
Of fabric subtly spun,
Knowing those colors cannot fade
That never feel the sun.

MOVING SNOW

Feet that have walked in moving snow,
Whether on a familiar street,
Or a whitened road they do not know,
Have performed the office of feet.

Mission has called them; from the dark
Of walls they have turned and sought the light,
And passing they have left a mark
Of a footprint on the white.

Whether with sober toe and heel,
Measuring out a chilly pace,
Or tripping a little for the feel
Of snowflakes lighting on a face—

They leave a peppered track behind,
And where each footstep's scar has been
For one sure moment well defined,
Patiently the snow drifts in.

Ahead of Him

He walks with a smile upon his lips,
As though he saw ahead of him
Something as pleasing as bright ships
Sailing an ocean's rim.

The pavement answers to his feet
With all the arrogance of stone,
And back of him the narrow street
Points out the path that he has known.

But he is immune to sound and sight,
So preoccupied is he
With something ahead of him, like bright
Ships on the rim of the sea.

A Whistler in the Night

Bright disks of sound
Spin through the air—
Metallic petals falling on the ground
From trees that bear
Somewhere in the spaces of the night.

Not petals, these
Spheres of tone;
But rounded luscious shapes of harmonies—
Like fruit, wind-blown,
Scattered wantonly upon the night.

Not shapes, but suddenly embodied song
With wings that lift
Into a throng
Of iridescent butterflies… and drift…
Into the nothingness beyond the night.

Sighers

A man may sigh as he goes by.
That may be all there is to it;
He gives a sigh and his troubles die,
Yet sometimes there is this to it:

A sigh, an echo thin as smoke
Lifting out of a crumbling pit—
A heart's wild cry worn to a sigh.
And that is all there is to it.

AT THE CORNER

Something is waiting for him at the corner,
And the street, like life, is a lonely place;
Though it is crowded no one can defend him
When he comes face to face
With what is waiting for him at the corner.

There may be something strange as a black man waiting
With a club that hurts like death, for his head;
Or a shrouded figure may slip from a doorway
And follow in his tread.
Certain it is that something is waiting at the corner.

And yet it may be only a smiling hour,
Like a girl with blossoms in her hair,
To slip an arm in his and walk beside him
Making him unaware
Of something that is waiting at the corner.

CROWDS

No wonder they who pass all day,
Like maskers in a masquerade,
Are always hurrying away
To where walls hold out quiet shade.
(Or else how poor were they!)
No wonder they would rest their eyes
Where only sightless shadows stir,
Flinging aside their thin disguise.
(Or else how poor they were!)
No wonder when the silence lies
In secret pools, untouched and dark–
Where only vagrant memory delves–
They poise like swimmers clean and stark,
And plunge into themselves.

WALKING

You I will follow;
Where your foot falls
There shall be my foot,
What mission calls
You is the mission
That urges my feet
Into the distance.

Now down the street
I am your shadow.

It is as I thought,
Your own motion drapes you
With dignity, caught,
A toga, at your shoulder.
And it is true
Your own footsteps herald
And beat drums for you.
As I knew it would be,
It is good to have pride
That is lift of a shoulder,
That is shout in a stride.

The air tempts your breathing,
As I knew it might,
Till each breath goes from you
Like wings in flight.
And no breath is wasted
Of breath that is sped
With the slow grace of sea birds
Over a head.

New streets are waiting
Beyond the turns;
At each street's ending
The distance yearns.

The way is less sober;
It wavers and after
A plunge, it flares up
In a ripple like laughter.
Then with the purpose
Of testing your skill,
It leaps before you
And calls with a hill.

But no hill can shame you,
The new demand
It makes upon you
Is a staff in your hand.

Here on the summit
The way is slow;
There is a feeling
Of trees. Below
The distance crouches.
Ahead, and side to side,
The yearn of all space reaches
Like great arms opened wide...
Shadows wrap about you,
Shadows that are made
Of wind and night reach for you,
Folding you into the shade...

I know now why you press on
Into a distance black
With formlessness; I know now
There is no turning back.

The Singing

Song is unrest;
It lives in the blood,
It flames in my pulses,
It rhythms this flood
Of people passing.

Quiet may sweep,
Water-slow, down my fingers,
Though my blood will not sleep.

The street may be cold stone,
Yet people sing by,
For the reason they live,
And the reason they die.

A Passer

I wonder as I watch you pass
Day after day,
Have you ever known the sink of grass
On an airier way?

You seem so reconciled to go
The grey way of a street,
And yet I think your footsteps know
A fuller beat.

For often as I am wondering,
And you go by,
I see you lift your eyes and fling
A recognition at the sky.

PURSUIT

She knows some one is following her–
Else why the commotion of her feet,
And why do her shrill heels cry and cry
To people passing: Quick! let me by?

She knows some one is following her
And fears to look backward down the street–
Else why does she always plunge ahead
Crying: Quick! let me pass! with her tread?

She knows some one is following her,
And: Mercy! Mercy! her footsteps beat.
Yet relentlessly her own Self steals,
Close as a shadow, forever at her heels.

A GOOD WALKER

When you walk up a street you breast the air
As bathers push the sea for love of it
And buoyantly yet guardedly submit
To hidden forces there.

It is as though you understand the tide
Of life that undulates about your tread;
You will not let it stay your course, instead
It gives your progress pride.

Before you, like the break of high tides, tower
Uncertainties you do not fear to meet,
Knowing that none can dispossess your feet
Of this deliberate hour.

MIDDLE-AGED

I know that you must come and go,
Woman of years, along my street.
I understand your step; I know
I should not listen to your feet
Thinking to hear accents of grace.
I know I should be glad to think
Of grey leaves breaking into space
After much thought of trees that blink
Their leaves, immobile in the sun.
I know, and you know, beauty dies
That it may live, that one by one
New splendors from the old may rise.
We know the hour of sun is worth
The realization of decay—
The old relinquishment to earth.

So, Woman, as you go your way,
Measure your tread out as you must.
Knowing these things shall you or I
Question the efficacy of dust?
Shall we not reason that life's cry
With all its fitfulness suppressed
Under the quiet of your tread
Has found rest from the old unrest
And has been wisely comforted?
Then pass on by before my ear
Catches your footsteps' lowest sound—
Pass on if I am not to hear
The truth your feet speak to the ground.

PROFIT

What if it were true, People,
And you were all you longed to be,
Could the earth be more than earth
Could the sea be more than sea?

Walk upon the world, People,
Follow green tides into space,
Then find your profit in a breath,
And in the light across your face.

MORE THAN SOUND

After you have passed, the silence
Grown from your echoed tread,
Is like a flower that is unfolding
In my hands.... Soft petals spread
Mistily across my fingers;
Dim leaves twine in cooling strands
About my wrists....
                    Your passing gives me
Quiet that fulfills my hands.

STRANGER

He has gone down the street, and I know he will
        not be back.
Our street was too walled a place, too tooled a track,
For him to find or to lose himself; he will not be back.

There was that in the ride of his shoulder and of
        his head,
That cried for the fumes of a background deeply red.
There was a demand for fullness in the breaking of
        his tread.

When I see him again I shall see him, not seeing him,
Carved black against the line of a hill's hot rim,
Finding and losing himself in the space that has
        lured him.

He Went By

He has a deft yet furtive way
Of balancing himself;
He walks as his wife on cleaning day
Dusts china on a shelf.

And Either Way

There is a day for me when every footfall
Is quieted as though in snow;
Another day is mine when sounds are waters
That clutch my throat and will not let me go.

The day that comes to wrap me in white silence
Gives me the sound of my own blood to hear,
And frail shadow that moving on my fingers
Becomes too intricately dear.

The day that beats against me, lifts me, bears me
Far out upon the tides of sound that race
More furiously than waters; I am stifled,
And lose myself within the thought of space.

NAKEDNESS

She has a way of being glad,
Of being glad that she has feet;
Of saying she will not be sad
So long as there remains a street
To be a welcome to her feet.

She says it with a parasol
And with a gown of rainbow plaid;
She boasts of it with heels; yet all
She tells is were she not so glad
It might be that she would be sad.

APRIL AGAIN

I shall not be singing
Of April this year,
And if there comes a footstep
I will not hear.

All my songs of April
Sing myself to me,
And every talking footstep
Tells of the hills or sea.

And I am tired of hearing
Things too often said.
So I will fold my fingers,
And I will bow my head.

To an Experienced Walker

Once when you walked through the spring
Birds had a swifter note,
And every flowered thing
Seemed quivering at your throat.

What is your April now
But time when leaves are new,
Spurting from every bough
With sunlight showing through?

And yet this much is good:
Knowing their powdery death
All leaves must serve your mood,
And none can hurt your breath.

NEW SPRING

It would be an unholy thing
Not to be glad when I am glad,
Today when feet have a song to sing,
And every bird in the sky is mad.

Not to be glad would be to lie
Quite dead, or wrapped in burning sleep,
Today when sounds so gaily die
For the sake of a singing echo, and I
Am so glad a thing that I could weep.

HE RAN PAST

I did not see you
As you ran past,
Yet for me your hurry
Must always last.
A flame where space
Forever calls,
The flight of an arrow
That never falls—
You are a motion
Over my mind.
The immobile darkness
Streaming behind
Backgrounds your swiftness.
I feel you run
As life would not let you,
Fairer than sun
Could ever paint you.
And with the flood
And fire of your going
You kindle my blood;
You warm me, then cool me
With continuous stride
Leaping into nothing
Like the wind at your side.

MATURITY

He is companioned secretly
When, with meditative feet,
He passes down an idle street.

A slow and misted company
Disputes his solitude. Ahead,
Like figures in a pageant, tread
All his tomorrows with eyes that peer
Over the near horizon's rim.
He cannot hear above the dim
Sound of their feet; he cannot clear
His thought from the restricting gaze
Fastened upon him from behind,
Where follows the gracelessly resigned
Figures of his yesterdays.

FOOTFALLS

I

Life, be my pillow.
Forget, forget, forget
If I once asked for wandering
With never a thought of cold or wet.
Forget, forget, forget, forget
If I once asked for roads that fled
Before resisting tread.
Be nothing for my feet, life;
Be something under my head....

II

I have loved,
And having loved, walk well.
I move not as I once, a lover, moved,
For now no stammered gladness of the mind
Corrupts my step's tonality; a bell,
Well-rung, is not more finally resigned.
With all that once was love I feed my feet.
Hear in my tread assimilated need;
Hear reaching, yielding, tempered to the beat
Of tethered rhythm; hear my sounds succeed
Each other, dying away
Into the day....

III

Motion, motion;
Life is meaningless
Save in its motion.
I will move, blind; I will feel nothingness,
So that, itinerant, I may unwind
Meanings coiled in my feet. And though there be

Only the meaning of futility,
Yet, moving, I shall find
All that is ever found:
Motion, and echoed motion,
Sound....

IV

Away,
Look away from me, away.
Consider how the pools of sun
Glisten in paleness on the street, and know
That I deplore with you what is begun
Only to serve the purpose of decay.
Consider well the daylight's watery glow
Shed by a sun involved in its more slow
Manner of dissolution, so that I,
Unheeded, may pass by....

V

We live, we die,
Of course we die,
For we have lived and all
That pushes toward the sky
Must, after reaching, fall.
So if we live today
We may not live tomorrow,
Yet there's a better way
To die than to die of sorrow.
And whatever the dying be,
Companioned by winds that stalk
Beside us undyingly,
Let us walk, walk....

VI

Hear me, I am guilty,
I am guilty, guilty, guilty.
My foot is heavy with the crime
Of going; I am guilty, guilty.
Hear me, and deplore what Time,
As its accomplice, makes me be,
For Time has made a tool of me,
And I am guilty, guilty, guilty.
Hear me, I am compelled to move,
To inflict my dream, to spend my love
And all the essences of life
Furthering strife....

VII

Lost,
Lost, perhaps my way;
Perhaps the roads that crossed
Muddled my feet; perhaps a ray
Of light that I was meant to see
To make intelligible to me
The sense of something lost, is lost.
Lost, perhaps a wind-snatched word
Yet to be heard....

VIII

Flame might follow my feet
Were I one motion nearer fire.
I am so nebulous with heat,
So much a shaping of desire,
Flame might follow, might follow my feet.
A dripping wing of flame might fuse
With my shadow but for the street
Cooling my shoes....

IX

On and on;
I must go on and on
Through noon and night and dawn.
Only this is given me:
The going on and on and on
Through noon and dusk and night and dawn;
Never the interval to be
The contour of myself. With sound
Leaning like rain above the ground,
I must go on and on: a shape
Existent in escape....

X

The tip of a fir,
And it is colored green,
Over a shiny roof is seen.
And who needs more, even if there were
Something more than the tip of a fir?
And who would think, even if they could,
Of roots and trunks that have stood, have stood
Through—but who would care how many springs—
Even if there were such things?
Over a roof
The feathery green
Tip of a fir
Is seen,
Seen....

XI

Love me,
Love me; life am I,
And time is relentless lullaby.
Love me, touch me; my hands make
Your hands whole and keep you awake.

Touch me, lead me where high walls keep
Back the winds that might sing of sleep,
Yet never so far that slow desert sands
Swirl in our eyes and quiet our hands,
And never and never into the mist
Drowsy with sea. Hear the blood in my wrist
Evolving sound to chasten the tune
Time has sung to the moon....

XII

Listen,
Listen, listen, listen.
Spend your hearing listening
To the utterance of my feet—
Utterance of my feet, my feet.
Deafen yourself on the sounds I fling
Bountifully over your dismal street,
And make them do for a quieter day
When I may not pass this way.
Listen, though you break your ear;
Listen, and you will hear
My feet, my feet, my feet....

XIII

I must not sound.
Softness, be between me and the ground.
Caution, be my sandal, let me pass
Unchronicled like feet that fall on grass.
There has been much to chasten and to shame
Along the never-ending way I came;
There is so much of hush, of sleep in me
That once was wildness, I move quietly.
And yet for all my care I sound, I sound;
Like a panther through a tangled ground
I sound....

XIV

Nothing,
Hear no more than nothing.
Hear no less, for that am I.
I am all that and yet no more
Than shadow on a wall, a high
Flurry of sand that swirls because
The wind has moved it from a shore
To fling it back to quietness.
No more, no more than this: the pause
Of many silences, no more,
And yet no less,
No less....

THE PATRICIAN

If culture had fluidity
It would drip from her finger-tips like rain,
And where it spattered there would be
Indelible purple stain.

If quietude had tongue what speech
Would iterate above her head,
What clamorous echoes would beseech
Behind her quiet tread.

But spent blood leaves no stain nor stir,
Save in that art which marks her ways—
The background dead hands make for her
With their defeated days.

INCIDENTAL

How can I rid me
Of what is not mine:
This self that was youth's,
This song swift and fine
That wraps me with fire,
And yet is not mine?

Song to be seemly
For her that is I,
Is song low with sleep
To be hummed in a sigh,
As I weave cool reason
Out of sounds that go by.

And who would be wanting
Song not her own,
Though it warms with warmth
The sun has not known,
When she might be thinking,
And cold and alone?

An Old Man's Walk

His slow steps feel along the street.
Upon a quest beyond his scope,
And one he has forgot, his feet
Must blindly grope.

His hands have given up and weigh,
Disillusioned, on a cane,
Scarred with the old desires that they
Snatched at in vain.

The question of his eye has stilled,
Though yet unanswered, his wet gaze
Is stagnant with the unfulfilled
Dreams of other days.

And yet the quest of life concerns
His tread; with effort vague and thinned
As a drift of smoke that turns
A little while before the wind–

He moves along a darkened rim,
Like a fissure yawning in the street,
While the life that has eluded him
Still tempts his feet.

The Flower of Illusion

Of course it's rather heavy, dear—
This something that you thought to wear
Like a red flower pinned in your hair.
Less like illusion and more like fear
It weighs upon you now, poor dear.

You thought that this was something you
Could wear until the dimmest days.
Now in your pretty hair it weighs
As a flower was never meant to do.
Of course it's heavy, poor dear you.

A Man Goes By

Where his sure feet pass
The crowds are strangely thinned;
They are the furrowed grass
And he is the wind.

Many go with the thought
Of their footfall's little beat,
Wearing their own lives caught
Like shackles on their feet.

But his mind is not led
Along a footstepped way;
There is motive in his tread
That was not shaped from clay.

Thresholds may make him small,
But the wind is in his feet–
Dominant, impersonal,
As he walks upon a street.

WHERE OTHERS WALK

Life is such music in her ear
Her feet are made to subtly dance
Where others walk with heavy feet, and hear
Only the deafening whir of circumstance.

Where others walk, she moves as trees
Sway, when the wind is low and sweet,
Making creation's unheard harmonies
Visible with the motion of her feet.

BRACKEN

Woman, if some one from your house had died
Would you not put a flower on his grave?
Yet when youth died in you—
The best friend you ever knew—
Did you, in memory of its cleanly pride,
So much as keep the dead leaves off its grave?

Dearer than father, mother, sister, lover,
Youth died in you and made your body a grave.
And yet day after day
You go your sleepy way—
Blind to the creeping weeds that soon may cover
What might have been a green and useful grave.

October Window

Words drift between me and the street,
Torn words of song that swirl like brown
And yellow leaves about the feet
Of people passing up and down.

With purpose hurt as a broken stem,
With music lulled to drifting sighs,
Whimsically the wind sweeps them
Across my eyes,

And flings them, always like a brown
Flurry of leaves, along the street,
Where mistily they are trampled down
Under the quiet thud of feet....

Torn words go from me in the mood
Of time, and gently cease to be,
And yet I find their passing good
So dreamfully they go from me.

EPHEMERA

There is a woman who makes my eye
A place of shadows, as now and then
I see her dimly going by,
And faintly coming back again.

She moves as many others move;
There is no utterance in her tread
To tempt an echo, nor to prove
What other footsteps have not said.

As often as she comes and goes
She is forgotten, as now and then
The wind is forgotten until it blows
A blur of dust down the street again.

The Hurrier

He is so bitterly concerned
With time, he takes no pride
In going where his steps are turned,
Nor in the manner of his stride.

He finds discomfort in his powers
Of hurrying up a street,
And yet he hurries on. The hours
Are spaniels snapping at his feet.

He Walked On

Walk, walker, that you may stamp out,
With the pressure of your walking feet,
The lines of unrest that track your brow
Like muddy footprints on the street.

Walk on, walk off the questioning
Of uneasy feet; walk to repress
Not only your footsteps but the pang
Of more enduring restlessness.

Time your feet of life to ease
Concern with immortality;
As too much wind, or too much rain,
Dulls an old longing for the sea.

ARRAIGNED

I am arraigned in listening to feet:

You who have listened long have heard us not,
Calling us fugitive names like rain, like sleet,
Saying that we are leaves the wind forgot.

Do you not remember?
                              Give us our due.
But for the thunder breaking from our tread
The silence would be softly deafening you,
And you be threading a needle with a thread.

Do you not remember?
                              Admit that we
Have quieted your fingers, flung a light
Across your mind by day and soothingly
Have wandered through your heart when there was night.

To One Coming in Sight

If you will pass with your eyes before you,
With motion narrowed as a flame,
I will not let my eyes assail you
To censure or acclaim.

You have a right to pass unquestioned,
Shaking the sounds off your feet
Like drying sand, and be forgotten
Along our quiet street.

You have this right, yet have it only
So long as you let your body be
What your shadow is that moves beside you:
A thing of blowing symmetry.

Echoes of Her

Brown roads have been too muddy,
Gold roads have been too bright,
And wind and moon and starshine
Have hurt my rest by night....

The flowers that they bring me
Will wither–Oh, I know!
And they will freeze in winter
Laid on the hard cold snow.

THE HIPPITY-HOPPER

I saw you go by
And I saw in your face
More than I heard
In the rigid grace
And dance of your hippity-
Hoppity pace.

Child, too many
Have passed as you do;
You tell of the many
And nothing of you:
What many have done,
What many will do.
Yet for all the archaic
Accents you speak
I am permitted
To see in the streak
Of sunlight that makes
A bronze of your cheek,
Something immobile
For all that you move
As transient as wind.
And for all that you prove
Nothing endures
For me you prove
A static symbol.
And strange, child, strange,
That my idea of you
Owes nothing to change,
While you must be prey
To life's wasting range.

Light strikes you to bronze,
And forgetting the rhyme
And trite rhythm you use,
I would sing you to time—
In syllabled sculpture
Give you to time.

Epitaph for a Neighbor

He lived because he found himself with breath.
He laughed, he thought, he walked down many a street;
Laughed less, thought less, and walked with slower feet.
He died because he lost himself in death.

Today

Let them go by; I will not hear.
I am tired of the bells in their feet
Ringing ceaselessly: near, far, near.

Let their sounds stay down in the street;
Let them go north, let them go south,
And stop this curving up a stair
To fling an echo upon my mouth
And to move like wind against my hair.

As She Passes

She has beauty, she has youth.
What is time, what is truth?

Her tread sings along the street.
What are old and groaning feet?

Life, a lover suave and gay,
Companions her upon her way.

He whispers of a tryst tomorrow.
What is betrayal, what is sorrow?

They Will Come

They will come, at last they will come, who have not
        gone by:
The many that time and life have not yet defined.
Even now the sound of their tread is a cry
Moving along my mind.

They will come and like mist be blown down a
        shadowy street,
Even as others have come and were mistily blown.
They will move to music of unisoned feet,
Yet each, like others, alone.

Their eyes will be sharpened as eyes of the others were
        not;
They will see in the sun, hear more in the wind than
        sound.
They will feel in the cold crusts of earth the hot
Desires of the ground.

All that others have known of longing and pain
Will be immeasurably theirs; they must reckon and face
Rapture unknown, then pass like the rain
Drifting on into space.

Prayer Against Triteness

There should not be singing
In my blood today;
I should lock my fingers
Like one who would pray,
And shape a thought to quiet
What my lips might say.

I should pray to Silence
When sounding in my veins
Is the one song, the long song,
Heard in leaning rains
And every step whose echoes
Break on windowpanes.

O Silence, lend my singing
What was never heard;
Let me taste the sweetness
Of breath as yet unstirred,
That I may cry out with the cry
Of your unuttered word.

THE PITY OF IT

If a wind blew up the street,
Wind that was never known,
Wind to annihilate feet,
To break and crumble stone;

And after the wind the sea
Came unendingly in,
And all of earth would be
As it had never been;

The intellect that is
Bone-frail would then be spent,
Not sharpened and tinged by this
Incomparable incident.

His Eyes Are on the Ground

You, who walk with eyes upon the ground,
I do not hear you pass, I feel instead
A fine contempt for all the narrow sound
Falling like clotted dust from passing tread.

The manner of your moving eases me.
You seem to walk between me and the sun
Which wraps you now with dangerous radiancy
Like flames that burn and blacken as they run.

And yet you move with unconcern, and I
Am pleased with you, though I know not how far
Your thought resists the menace in the sky,
Or if you but forget that such things are.

SELF INQUISITION

Who is this who affects a window,
Paning her eyes with blue of glass,
Feeding her ears on luscious wisdom
And vanity of those who pass?

Knows she no glass save that shimmers
With rain, or where the sunlight lies—
Are there no panes more subtly lighted
On the far side of her eyes?

Knows she no sound save whose echoes
Footprint the dust—what of the tones
Beyond her hearing, cool, enduring,
As water falling over stones?

A pane of glass across her vision,
A wind of sound against her ears,
Is healthy only if it sharpen
More than she sees, more than she hears.

PEDESTRIAN

Did you have a yesterday—
Do you look for a tomorrow?
Curious, you exist for me
Only in the infectious sorrow
Of your passing. Unyesterdayed,
Untomorrowed, you pass by,
And in the lingering tragedy
Of a moment, live and die.

THE THIN DOOR

When you have walked where you would walk,
And tired your feet of streets and lanes,
Behind a thin door you will talk
Of what you know of suns and rains.

Much you will tell of cooling fact.
You will name the hours dawn and noon,
Predict how all the stars will act
And where the sky will wear the moon.

Yet there will be what you cannot say
Hardened in thought, as in a mine
Lies the unlighted ore; today
Has held more than you can define.

What you may tell is the desperate reach
Of tongues now satiate with clay,
And what will glitter beyond your speech
Is what an unshaped tongue will say.

PROTECTION

I have envied, I have pitied,
Wrapped their sorrows over me
Like a shawl, to keep from knowing
Cold that is colder than the sea.

I have raised my face to ice winds
That froze the laughter in their eyes,
Heard the break of storm that bowed them
With the wisdom of its cries.

And the black storm and the whirlwind
That have made them wise and old,
Even so have worn and shaped me,
And have wrapped me from the cold.

He Walks with His Chin in the Air

Life in you is an incurious madness.
Tell me, how good is life that is not known
And is but felt, like wind against the temples,
Like touch beneath the feet, of turf or stone?

But do not hear me, lover of life; an answer
Is burning like a sorrow in my breast:
There is flame in feeling, fineness in the knowing,
And who shall say which way of life is best?

Pass on, seeker, seeking the touch of spaces.
Many the ways of life, and many a one
Is all too brief a fluttering of hours
To serve our purpose here beneath the sun.

APATHY

One by one you follow
After the manner of sheep,
Follow the way that leads you
Into a place called sleep–
Drowsily, drowsily follow,
Men and women like sheep.

Oh, you who levelly follow,
Have you never climbed a height?
Does some one not remember
A weeping in the night?
Then for the glittering sake of it,
If ever you sorrowed or sinned–
For the sake of one who is listening,
Turn, and follow the wind!

WALKER OF NIGHT

I feel the leash-like straining of his motion
Though so quietly he moves
Through darkness tangled as the midnight ocean.
Steadily he moves,
And move against him ropes of shadow, breaking
His progress, tethering him to night.
Oh, I fear for his desperate undertaking
To walk the depths of night.

SANITY

If I could look into your eyes,
Out of their blackest depths I think
That I might draw, as from a well,
Something of you for me to drink.

Others have passed and been as bread
Held to my mouth, others as wine,
But as you pass an older want
Becomes less definitely mine.

The passion of the sun has filled
Your eyes, and filtering, has wrought
A clarity in you that is
A drink of water to my thought.

The wind has followed with its ice.
Now of the flame, the frost, you hold
Reflection that glitters in your eyes,
And is not warmth and is not cold.

Songs To Be Said While Walking

I

Let the day come out of the night
And the night come out of the day–
Night from day, and day from night,
And let the hours be a flight
Or wild birds winging away.

And whether the night or whether the day,
As the hours forever fly,
Holding the sun on their wings, or grey
With the dusk of night, let them go their way
Calling across the sky.

II

Love cannot stay, love cannot pass.
For every love that dies,
Swift as a flower from the grass,
A newer love shall rise.

Then why have I so long a face,
And why are you so proud?
For one the spring comes on apace,
For one, the snow's white shroud.

III

We may wander and wander far,
Wander far as the blue hills are;
Yet never so far as the blue hills seem–
Oh, the blue of a hill is a mist, a gleam,
Lighting a face, cooling the mind.
And though the roadways wind and wind,
And though we follow and wander on
Always the blue grows green as a lawn;
And always, though roads run green, run high,
Blows a blue mist across the eye.

Through the Rain

Passers, pass me like the rain.
Be shadow shapes that curve and lean
With every turn of wind; refrain
From being felt and being seen.

Walk less and drifting more, go by
Unheard or with the certain sound
Of water slanting from the sky
And falling softly on the ground.

Be meaningless; over my mind
Blow like gusts across the pane.
Leave me alone and free to find
The cooler meaning of the rain.

These Who Pass

Who would pity these who pass:
Many whose blood time has made thin,
These who are too frail to sin?
Who would pity these who pass
Gently through the sun to find
Nothing there to heat the mind?
To them night comes unstrange and deep,
To them the dew on darkened grass
Smells only of the dusk of sleep.

And who would pity these who pass:
Many whose firm veins run with fire,
To whom life is unshaped desire?
Who would pity these who pass
With the insinuating sun
Moving against their flesh? Not one
But in his hunger fully lives,
But, thirsting, drinks from the gilded glass
Of life, as much as living gives.
Who would pity these who pass?

HUNGER

I have known life's hunger,
Though by other name;
It has been dream and singing,
Faith and the whip of shame.

Not until I listened
To sounds of a world swept by,
Did I learn to hear my own heart
And hear all life in its cry.

Not until the hunger
Of all the world was blown
Like a wind against my window,
Could I name my own.

And I have learned that only
This is not proved vain:
Hunger by which a world is fed
As I am fed by pain.

TO AN UNPLEASED PASSER

Is there a long hill
Where you would be,
That moves down softly,
Green and gold, to the sea?

Is there a mountain,
Wedded to time,
And ridged with crystal
That you would climb?

Or have you longing
Undefined,
Fretting like a shadow
Your surface of mind,

That feeds on darkness
And the pain of your breast,
And shoes your feet
With dumb unrest?

THEY WHO WALK IN MOONLIGHT

Walk softly through the moonlight,
Softly, lest the sound
Startle the silver on your ankle
And strew it ash-like on the ground.

If you have burning in you
A tinge of thought more bright
Than is the moonlight's sulphur color,
Do not walk tonight.

They walk best in moonlight
Who borrow for their own
The passion of the moon to keep them
Impersonal as stone.

They who walk in moonlight
Should be so drunk with death
They pour themselves out in libation,
Breath on radiant breath.

Summary

They are always looking for what they never find.
With eyes eager for sky they look ahead,
Mirroring for a moment the color of space.

They are always seeking a road to vividly wind
Out of the ways that have tamed and hurt their tread.
It is always before them like wind that brushes the face.

I am always looking for what I never find;
Peering and crying into my heart, I seek
The breath that is made of fire which shall fulfill.

I am always hungering for the undefined
Taste of a word I have not learned to speak.
My breath is wasted flame, my lips are still.

We are always seeking, and when we do not find,
One by one, we see the symbol of things
In the sky's illusion of light, in the wind's rebuff.

One by one, in the refuge of the mind,
We strive to give the understanding wings
And to make the brilliant flight of it enough.

CRY OF TIME

CRY OF TIME

For this there is no sound;
For this I cannot shape
Utterance to escape
Air where my breath is drowned.

So small a space it moves,
This, my cry of time;
No stronger than a rhyme
Its strength of being proves.

Lying at my throat,
Secret and unbroken,
It seemed its crying, spoken,
Might leap with arrowed note.

Into fluid light
Its baffled meanings run,
Made beautiful as the sun,
Equivocal as night.

I who strive for word
That will define like death,
Nourish a little faith
In the silence that is heard.

HERE COMES THE THIEF

Here comes the thief
Men nickname Time,
Oh, hide you, leaf,
And hide you, rhyme.
Leaf, he would take you
And leave you rust.
Rhyme, he would flake you
With spotted dust.
Scurry to cover,
Delicate maid
And serious lover.
Girl, bind the braid
Of your burning hair;
He has an eye
For the lusciously fair
Who passes by.
O lover, hide—
Who comes to plunder
Has the crafty stride
Of unheard thunder.
Quick—lest he snatch,
In his grave need,
And sift and match,
Then sow like seed
Your love's sweet grief
On the backward air,
With the rhyme and the leaf
And the maiden's hair.

To an Indolent Woman

Dusk with never a wing to make
A pointed shadow on the grass,
Prepares a darkness that will break
Above you like a dome of glass.

If you had drunk from scented air
Until you breathed yourself alive,
Smoothing your eyes on silver where
The birds that make the twilight dive,

Night would be taut above your head,
And dark, like split glass, purple and blue,
Like twisted iron and splintered lead,
Would not crash down, dispersing you.

And when your body curved to rest,
A rhythm slow as the wing of a gull,
Moving in quiet through your breast,
Might make your slumber beautiful.

BIRD AT DAWN

Now it is to be,
This that was never known:
Light lifts from the tree
Of dark. When it has flown,
Beating a great white wing
Over the chronic night,
There will be no thing
But will come alive with light.
Stillness, anciently long,
Will break when delicate mirth
And love tremble to song
And curve the throat of the earth.

BEFORE QUIET

I will think of water lilies
Growing in a darkened pool,
And my breath shall move like water,
And my hands be limp and cool.

It shall be as though I waited
In a wooded place alone;
I will learn the peace of lilies
And will take it for my own.

If a twinge of thought, if yearning
Come like wind into this place,
I will bear it like the shadow
Of a leaf across my face.

HAND IN SUNLIGHT

This is my hand I lift to you;
It is not whitened leaf, O Sun.
And these thin cords of quivering blue
Lacing the pulse, are veins that run
Beneath the flesh to make it white.
These are my fingers, not twigs pale
From too long hanging in the light.
Supple as reed yet firm as mail,
They droop but for a shape of ease,
Are quiet for the sake of fine
Shadows that rim them and increase
The accuracy of their design.
You are but background; you are spun
From tinsel in a glittered mesh.
My hand stands out like white bronze. Sun,
I shame you with my tepid flesh.

Audience to Poet

Poet with the pointed breath,
Who matches darkness of the mind
With syllables so taut they wind
Their meaning in a living death,

Spare us no twinge or brilliance stirred
With rapiers of speech that move
To break the dark from cool new love
Encompassed in the burning word.

That we may live enough to feel
Living, with something more than heart,
Lay on our eye your tonic smart,
Clang in our ear your uttered steel.

THE RAVELLING TUNE

She sews the morning hours away,
She sews away the noon;
She sews as glittering seasons pass—
June, October, June.
And as her needle runs she sings
A little ravelling tune—
She sings a ravelling tune.

She sings with words as light as breath
And soft as April rain,
And of the song she sings none hears
More than the thin refrain—
The ravelling refrain:
O some may sew for love's own sake,
And some must sew for pain.

Below the world of life moves by
As life must ever move—
Must ever, ever move,
Yet still her needle runs and still
The sun wheels by above.
O some must live for sorrow's sake
And some may live for love.

The seams she does not sew today
Another day will borrow,
And as her flashing needle runs
Today, and so tomorrow—
Tomorrow and tomorrow,
She sings a little ravelling tune:
For love or else for sorrow.

To a Poet Who Said Too Much

You have tired me with your words.
Words that once were radiant things,
Words that were smothered cries, were whips,
The quiver of fire, the call of birds,
Now have an utterance that flings
A taste like dust upon my lips.

You have hurt me with your rhyme;
It is a bell that has rung too long.
My ear is hungry for a word
Without a haunting, hollow chime.
I am thirsty for an unwooed song
That shall be felt and never heard.

Your lines are swarms of narrow bees
Spreading above my hive of thought
The droning of their baffled flight.
Now is no pang of breathing; these
Slow moments know no quiet caught
To sudden sound, no shaft of light.

Admonition Before Grief

Let the night weep on your hand;
Let the night's tears, dark and fine,
Slip down your fingers; understand
This grief is neither yours nor mine.

There is a reason for the night.
Why weep for dark so luminous
That it is only tempered light?
Rather the night must weep for us.

Reach out your fingers to the cold
Blackness of space before tomorrow;
Lift up your hand and night will hold
And cool it with its lovely sorrow.

White Branches

I had forgotten the gesture of branches
Suddenly white,
And I had forgotten the fragrance of blossoms
Filling a room at night.
In remembering the curve of branches
Who beckoned me in vain,
Remembering dark rooms of coolness
Where fragrance was like pain,
I have forgotten all else; there is nothing
That signifies—
There is only the brush of branch and white breath
Against my lips and eyes.

A Child Is Lost

Perhaps the night wind will be tender
And will minister to her,
And the moon will come to send her
Light to see a twisted fir.
(The clouds are thick and do not stir.)
Stars may strew the black road over,
Tinting it bit by darling bit.
(The skies are low and still unlit.)
And the wild dark may but love her
Who knows no ill of it.

YOUR AUDIENCE

Poet, your utterance becomes my breath.
The rhythm of my pulses is the song
That burned in yours when once your blood was flame
And sang an hour of silence into fire.
Then, if your breath is mine, your singing mine,
Mine, too, the swift surrender to your whim
That is laughter on the lips of truth; and mine
The crying of your feet, and mine your eyes
Seeking to cool their sight upon horizons
Where minarets may justify the sun.

Poet, giving me breath,
The secret fury of your silences,
The password of your fancy that unlocks
Gates lightly swung upon the hinge of space,
Giving me your abandonment of time,
You lay your poem in my lifted hands.

Poet, now it is mine.
It has been sung and is for you a spent
Passion—a white smoke moving on the sky.
It has appeased your singing heart and given
Your feet a faith for having wandered well.
Then wrap the folds of your accomplishment
In a cloak about your sated shoulders; know
For you it is a journey old and done,
For me, a calling. Go, leave me alone
To live the wonder you have given me.

The names of places that are named with music
Shall be the singing signposts where I go.
And coolly and forever unamazed
I will find roads to tangle with my feet—
Roads intricate, ironic—roads and roads
To thirst for, thrill for, sing for, live for—die.
And I will be forever undismayed
At moonlit eyes, at tropical descents
And lightly ancient follies at my lips.
For my ignorance shall be split by screeching birds,
My innocence dissolved into the spray
Of cataracts and rivers leaping past...

Poet, well may you mourn,
And wrapped in heavy robes of your fulfillment,
Well may you envy me my unspent tread,
Envy my colored days, my tempted nights.
For you there is a journey old and done,
For me, a calling, and my breathing answer
That is an everlasting restlessness.

BLUE HILLS

There were eyes before mine
That lifted to the hills,
And drank from their blue distance
The quiet that fulfills.

You who found appeasement
In the hills' deep blue,
Has the final darkness
Brought wiser rest to you?

WHITE DAY'S DEATH

Light that streams into the grass
In white rain, light that fills a tree
With radiance like steel, like glass,
Makes me catch my breath to see.

Down, down it pours in cold sun, thinned
To web of crystal; streak on streak
It falls, chastening the wind
And making every small bird meek.

Farther into the ground's black space
Recedes earth's little warmth; earth grown
Unfecund, now is made a place
Of brittle dust and stone.

Silver filters through my eye
Until my very brain is lit
With the glitter of sterility
That is both grave and exquisite.

INHERITANCE

Over and over again I lose myself in sorrow;
Whatever I have borne I bear again tenfold.
The death of sorrow is a sleep; a newer sorrow
Wakes into flame from ashes of the old.

They said that sorrow died and that a sorrow buried
Made your mind a dear place like a grave with grass,
Where you might rest yourself as in a willow's
        shadow,
And cold and clean, might feel the long world pass.

But sorrow does not die, sorrow only gathers
Weight about itself—a clay that bakes to stone.
When your own share of sorrow has worn itself to
        slumber
Then every woman's sorrow is your own.

For a Broken Needle

Even fine steel thinly made
To hold a raging thread,
Comes to lie with purple shade
In a dreaded bed.

All its chiseled length, its nice
Grip, its moving gleam
That was once like chips of ice
In a heated seam,

Are no more. It is fit
We should chant a strain
Of lament, then tumble it
Out into the rain.

Wild Geese

There was a throb of singing
Warm upon my mouth,
But I have seen the wild geese
Flying south.

I have heard them calling
From a leaden space,
And like a wind their cold cry
Has swept my face.

TO ALL QUIET PERSONS

Come out into the sunlight, come.
Waiting your foot the loam
Fluid with brilliance that will splash
Gilt on your instep, spray your eyes
With jetted light to make them flash
Gladness where they were only wise.

Come now, not soon, into the day
That is a glittering way
Hung with shapes casting no shade,
So verdant with the sun that space
Is a luscious radiance and made
An unbelievable orchard place.
Go where you will, do what you do,
Light like branches will cover you,
Like golden fruit hang over you.

You have only to come to be
Of all your wise selves free;
Only to come to rid your ankles
Of that blue cold that ever rankles
Like a purple shadow under flesh;
Only to come to taste the fresh
Fruits of the air and touch the breeze
As you might touch light leaves on trees
And pluck and scatter them as you please.
You have only to come to wear
Lovely things you have never worn,
Gay and glistening scarfs of air
So fragile they are never torn;
Only to come to feel the sweet
Smells of the earth against your mouth
And to hear drowned out in your own blood's beat

Wind of the north, breeze from the south.
And yet this much you will have to do;
The sun will not come in for you.
Is it so much to come, to come?
Waiting for you there is breath to sway
In unison with the drunken hum
Of sun-mad bees and the gold of day,
You have only to come.

INCANTATION

Give me words to please my tongue
And words in futile strands
Like colored beads, to twine among
The shadows in my hands.

Give me words like instruments
Of steel, to probe my mind,
That I may name its impotence
The small dark of the blind.

Give me words at night to calm
Like herbs; these I shall keep
Pressed to the cheek hot on my palm
To thinly scent my sleep.

THE SEA

Poets have talked too much about the sea.
Let who would speak of water tell of ways
A river follows, be concerned with haze
Of a dark lake where soon the dawn will be.
Let them, for beauty's aching sake, beware,
Who stand upon the sands in rich amaze,
Of shaping with the mouth a worded phrase,
Lest their thin breath should stain intrinsic air.

If they must cry the sea, the sea, what of
The silence that is beauty's very heart?
What magic will the word hold for tomorrow?
They will have sons who might have known the smart
Of sea song in their blood like joy, like sorrow,
And breathed the better for the secret love.

INLAND

Sea, I have sworn never to sing of you.
Come inland, Sea, come drench my little words
In dark fog like your narrow-bodied birds
With long hushed wings are ever flying through.
Snatch up my cries and break them as you do
Foam into spray. Oh, I know it would be
A glorious thing for words to drown in sea,
Sharing an eloquence they never knew.

But here, Sea, where the need of you is known
As thirst is known, a cry of song may reach
With any sultry breath to any sky.
Sea, let me not forget to learn the tone
Of soundlessness, to nurture secret speech
Before I shape my great love in a cry.

Weeper in the Dark

Be thankful, weeper in the dark, for tears.
Cherish each oval spark
Of moisture that upon your lash appears
To be a small defiance to the dark.

Make cups of both your hands, feel cool tears fall
Upon your palm's hot skin,
And know you hold the essences of all
The worth of you though piety or sin.

Be thankful that the full breath still may run
Distilling itself in tears for you to weep.
Better to grieve than smile into the sun
Like one who smiles in sleep.

October Chorus

Come not here to listen,
Come not here to see;
We but sing a broken song
Of a leaning tree.
We but sing a frail song
Like a leaf to droop
A moment over dark earth.
Feel a great tree stoop
With the weight of splendor.
Come not here for grief
And come not for gladness.
Feel the hanging leaf,
Twisted and discolored
Where it once was fair.
Know the feeling of the branch
That quivers on the air.

WINTER REST

Not for any troubled reason
Are words sweet upon my tongue,
Not for branches, bowed and silken,
Where once blossoms faintly clung;

Not for brittle leaves whose falling
Made pale sorrow of a stone,
But for sake of streaming fingers,
For unhungered flesh and bone.

There are words that sound like water
Dripping where the grass is deep;
These are mine for sake of singing
My long hands to sleep.

He Walked on Leaves

He wore a cryptic sadness for the year,
For he had seen two leaves break on the stem
And he had seen the wind take after them
As if it could not get enough of leaves.
And I who watched, was it through tear and tear
I saw him roughly button up his coat
To keep the wind from coming near his throat,
Or was it with that scrutiny that believes
In hiding in the blankness of an eye
What glitter lies beyond?
                              And he passed on,
And after him more leaves, crooked and wan,
Curved in more breaking patterns.
                                    Did I weep,
Or did I keep my eyeballs hard and dry
Like pebbles?
                Other winds moved up and down,
Cleaning the gutters that keep clean a town,
And other leaves came crookedly to sweep
The full light out and bring the half light in.

Twilight became a thing of broken leaves,
And every sound was like a bell that grieves
Over a stillness; life was little more
Than a distorted passion that had been.
Only remained the ways of leaves: the giving
To brittleness that which was soft and living,
Only the going on of him who wore
His collar up because he walked on leaves.
And covered with the gloom did I permit
My lowered lash to fringe with small beads lit

With evidence more visibly delicate
Than all the essence of the mind achieves?
Or did I round the pupil with a stare,
Keeping the lash as stiff as bracken where
The frost lies on it and the hour is late?

INCONTINENCE

Life is my lover;
I cannot rest
Save on his pillow,
Save on his breast.

When Life forsakes me
Then I will leap
To greet my new lover.
With Death I shall sleep.

PLEASANTRY

Never by a window,
Never near a wall
Troubled with a thousand shadows,
Have I watched the evening fall.

Never wall nor window
Had much to do with me—
I who had for gracious living
A hut beside the sea.

And when the half lights gather
Like a flock of narrow birds,
Think of me listening myself to death
On the ocean's mumbled words.

THE DUBIOUS SELF

Time will light a candle at your head,
Time will fold your hands across your breast.
Is it enough, the high and candled bed,
Enough that weary hands are caught in rest?

If it be not enough,
Shadowly lift upon your elbow, rise;
Fling out your arms, demanding for them love;
Demanding wrested beauty, lift your eyes.
Listen into the silences for sound
That made a music of your mind, and for
Your feet demand the sweet warmth of the ground,
For your too quiet hair, the wind once more.

And if it be enough,
Lie stiffly there, unmagical with death,
Forever losing sorrow, cleansed of love.
And on the dark will move the candles' breath.

HEALTH

I am stronger for having gone
Where I have never been.
I was nourished on milk of the dawn
That was mine for the drinking in.

I am better for what is mine
And for tonic of what I lack,
Better for the tremulous design
Of a leaf the moon made black.

Light Sleep

Women who sing themselves to sleep
Lie with their hands at rest,
Locked over them night-long as though to keep
Music against their breast.

They who have feared the night and lain
Mumbling themselves to peace
Sleep a light sleep lest they forget the strain
That brings them their release.

They dream, who hold beneath the hand
A crumpled shape of song,
Of trembling sound they do not understand,
Yet love the whole night long.

Women who sing themselves to sleep
Must lie in fear till day,
Clasping an amulet of words to keep
The leaning dark away.

HEAT

This is a quiet thing to say:
The sun is a yellow butterfly
Caught in the wind that is the day.
The wounded sun is carried high
Over the tops of the tallest trees
That mourn with sound like the voice of bees.
The sun is a butterfly, poor thing;
Soon it will fall with hanging wing
Into the blue earth of the west,
And night will come and I shall rest.

ELEVENTH MONTH

Now the time when winds may swoon
Before the stillness of the sun;
Early in the afternoon
The day grows dusky and is done.

Now the time when sharp hills fold
In space to lie forgotten there,
And slowly moving swords of cold
Split the heaviness of air.

If there is sound it is a sound
Made out of hush and shade; with these
It settles thickly to the ground
Like fog about the trunks of trees.

INTELLIGENCE

Whatever my thought has spun—
That spider refuting night—
What silver web in the sun,
What filmy meshes white
With dust, tangle in air.
What traceries are thinned
Leave a lost shape there
To curve with wind.

Caught against space they break...
A sparkle is gone like breath,
A dust settles for sake
Of logical smug death.
What contours, what hot rays,
Dissolve into the mist,
Serve to round my gaze
And heat my wrist.

RAIN

I have raised my hands to rain,
Raised my hands until my lifting
Fingers, like warm snow, seemed drifting
Into rain, becoming rain.

I have given all my hands.
Rain has taken them and made
Out of them a liquid shade
To lay upon a place of sands.

What stirred in my pulse now sighs
In the long sigh of the rain;
What was restlessness will rain
Against some woman's windowpane
And make a woman close her eyes.

What my fingers had of shape
Is a curve of blowing light,
Moving in unhurried flight,
With the rain, to its escape.

Yet what have I given rain,
Who have felt the edge of rain
Fray my fingers, who have striven
To give much, what have I given
But a little moving pain?

And what have I more, what boast
Of a meaning may I keep,
Who am weary as a sheep
And slightly pleasured like a ghost?

Tomorrow's Adventure

Low tide is the tide of sadness,
Yet I shall go down to the lowering sea,
And hold my two arms out in gladness,
Coaxing the sea to notice me.

Though fog may marry wave and boulder,
I will not hurry from the sands,
Though winds be whips upon my shoulder
They shall not flatten down my hands

Until I accuse the sea of sadness:
The time of sorrow, O sea, is when
You should profess untempered gladness.
Shall you never learn from the ways of men?

Of One Dead

They have made a quiet for him,
All the lovely dead who loved him
Have returned and move about him,
Cooling him with their pale shadows.

What in life they could not give him
Of their love they now bring to him,
Transmuted, so that it may serve him,
Into hush and drift of music.

Now one leaves the swaying circle,
Goes to him where he lies sleeping,
And the strangeness of her being
Like a moonlight, leans above him.

Sleep

There is a quiet where you go at night.
Your feet fall into earth cushioned like sands;
You part the waist-high poppies with both hands
And walk through dusk made purple with their light.
The poppies lay lush heads against your gown,
Leaving adoring stain; you do not know;
You do not feel the slanting of the slow
Rain of the twilight ever moving down.

An unconcern as tireless as a love,
Has wrapped a sultry darkness on your heart.
In some lost moment if your finger tips
Pressed back a petal, you know nothing of
The fervor of the touch, nor feel the smart
Of pollen that is dusky on your lips.

EXPERIENCED GRIEVER

Never say of me:
She had no tears to weep—
Her hard eyes knew but little more
Than brush of wind and sleep.

And never say of me:
Tears were in her eyes
Till, like a curtain, weeping hung
Across her dearest skies.

Say this: Her tears were plenty—
She wore them in her mind,
Where every one became a moon,
And terrible and kind.

THE SCARF

I have waked in the night to listen
In the greening of the year,
To the silken sound of raindrops
And found it good to hear.

I have caught the fluttered silence
To me like a soft shawl,
And lightly wrapped me in the comfort
Of hearing thin rain fall.

Every Day's Damocles

When dawn was tipping like a sword
Hung by a hair above your head,
Your eye's thick lid could ill afford
To lift so much as width of a thread.
You snuggled down into your bed.

In lights of steel the dawn stirred there
Until your cheek bone was outlined
With crystal and your coloring hair
Was streakéd like a melon's rind.
You would not let it tint your mind.

Blindly you turned as to a mother
To darkness that had been your foe.
You knew that there could be no other
To so appease your subtle woe.
Over you moved the day's white glow.

You breathed, and for your breath you found
Air like the waters of a lake,
And quivers of leaf and twittered sound.
You moved and thought your heart would break
Learning you were so soon to wake.

NEVER

They are singing me never-songs again.
Never, never, never
Cries every shadow dying of light;
Never, weep bells that ring in the night,
Never, never, never.

And this is the song that falls with the rain:
Forever, ever, ever;
Yet never tomorrow, never the dawn,
Never the music of earth moving on
Forever, ever, ever.

FOR A WOMAN GROWN COLD

Far as near things are when sleep
Blows over you like blackened sand,
Is the hot pain you thought to keep
Warm against your hand.

Grief left you colorless as stone.
You lie beneath night's splintering wave
That once you broke your heart upon
Dispassionate as in a grave.

You rise to face the sun and toss
The pleasure of it from your eyes;
Now will you think of dawns across
Your mouth, sweet with other skies.

You feel your thin blood pulsing where
It moves unheatedly as rain,
Content to find the chill breath there.
Cold is easier than pain.

Of Any Poet

After the song, there comes an hour
When Silence has its way with you.
It lays you out and puts a flower
In either hand; it lights a few
Gaudy candles at foot and head,
Then weeps, and you are very dead.

TRACT ON LIVING

Through hours woven of light and shade,
Where dawns, leaping a curve of hill,
Are gold too soon, and noons are made
To flash like waters of a rill;
Where dusk is blue upon the ground
And dark is arrowy with light,
Live, pretending you have found
Enough of day and night.

You may arise with the first slow
Shadow that moves the morning, go
Out to the hills, seeking the things
That may move near like indefinite wings
And seem, yet not seem, part of the mist
That is, yet is not, amethyst,
And is, yet is not, water-green,
But is a color felt, not seen.

Then loosen from your eyes the dawn,
Turn, and in your going tell
Nothing of ways that you have gone
To seek what seemed a moving bell
Muffled in distance. Where the day
Is shaped of splendor and all things sway
In a rhythm of light and sounds are long
With echo made of laughter and song,
You may seek once again the thing
You seek. Look well into the ring
Of arrogant glitter called the sun.
It may be something lightly spun–
A yellow web across black space,
Meaningless save to serve the hour
And be a pleasure on your face.

Or like a rocket it may shower
Wild color in your rounded eye,
Strewing a blindness through your head;
Yet let your turning manner cry
Of nothing save your tread.

After the dawn and after the noon,
Always there is the dusk, the moon.
Always the old ways new with dew,
Calling, calling, calling you:
Always the thing you seek so near
It is a part of what you hear
In the hushing grass, in the night hawk's note—
So near it is coolness on your throat
And curves of flame rounding your taut
Blue veins. Almost it seems that you,
The seeker, are the something sought,
Yourself the bell that called you through
The dawn, the noon, the dusk, the dew.
Almost it seems the tiger beat
Of your own pulses is the all,
The only answer is the call.

Night may become the mask of day,
A place of nothing, save a way
Where you must go pitting the light
Of self against the drench of night.
There you may find all things and none,
Yet let your turning step give sound
To nothing but the casual tone
Of feet upon the ground.
After the dusk, the blackened west,
Always there is the pillowed rest;

Always a hollow for your head
And for your body a clinging shape
Of quiet. Now your sleeping tread,
Poised, may be its own escape.
Now where the dark is drowsed with gold
And all the swarming gloom a curtained fold
Hanging between you and your quarrel of thought,
You may be filled with what you sought.

Maker of Songs

Take strands of speech, faded and broken;
Tear them to pieces, word from word,
Then take the ravelled shreds and dye them
With meanings that were never heard.

Place them across the loom. Let wind-shapes
And sunlight come in at the door,
Or let the radiance of raining
Move in silver on the floor.

And sit you quiet in the shadow
Before the subtly idle strands.
Silence, a cloak, will weigh your shoulder;
Silence, a sorrow, fill your hands.

Yet there shall come the stirring...Weaver,
Weave well and not with words alone;
Weave through the pattern every fragment
Of glittered breath that you have known.

For a Lost Grave

Who will be so quiet
Ever again,
As she beneath a riot
Of hard weed and rain?
None will have such sleeping,
None lie so alone.
Is there water seeping?
Is there sand or stone
To rattle when the wind blows?
None will lie so still.
Only the wind knows
The hollow or the hill.

INTERIM

I am weary of your talk of sorrow.
Sorrow is a word you must not say,
Not cry to night, nor whisper to the day.
Sorrow as a word is undefined;
It is a food, taste it and on the morrow
Tell nothing of the flavor of the rind.

I am weary of the thought of sorrow.
Sorrow is a thought I must not keep,
Not hold by day nor cherish through my sleep.
Sorrow is a feeling in my hand.
Then let me lock my knuckles and tomorrow
Speak not of what I do not understand.

Let us have nothing more to say of sorrow.
Our word's concern is but a twisted leaf
Blown down the shadowed verities of grief,
Falling into the silence whence it came.
Let us await the day after tomorrow
And lightly hear Time tell us sorrow's name.

COOLING SONG

Two lovely things, two green things—
Lay them on my eyes.
Find two leaves so narrow
They take you by surprise,
Leaves pointed like an arrow,
Soft as butterflies.

Two lovely things, two lean things—
Plucked where moons have bled
Grey light on the meadow
That was their wild birth-bed.
Find such subtle shadow
And bring it to my head.

Noon

This feather that is theirs to blow upon:
A pretty plaything known to each as breath,
This will be lost when the ample wind of death
Fans it along into an unlit dawn.
Yet why should there be care? Why need a wan
Hand supplicate, lest it be snatched too soon?
Why, like a fog, should chill fall on the noon
Because a feather dances and is gone?

The sun is in the sky. The distances:
The panting south, bright north, the east and west,
Are tonic for the lips, and there is strength
For limbs aspiring to such heights as these;
And there is laughter for the leaping breast
For all it lie unhumorous at length.

NIGHT

No one has seen the beauty of the night.
Many have stood under the moon and gone
Through lovely fogs of dusk until the dawn,
Always with blindness folded on their sight.
Many have worshipped there; many have poured
Their being out like water into sands;
Many have lifted timid lover hands,
And none has seen or known what is adored.

The monstrous beauty that is darkness blows
About them in a vapor; like linked steel
It fastens on their languid tread; they feel
Nearness of unimaginable repose,
That is no more than a shadow at the heel
Until there falls the darkness no moon knows.

THEY SAY HER HEART IS BROKEN

She is as heavy as so much sand;
She moves about like a moon, a mist.
Only her heart? Have you felt her hand?
Are fingers missing? Is it limp at the wrist?

Only her heart? How do you know
But what there is rattling in her head?
Only her heart? If that is so
Why such a looseness in her tread?

She comes, and you think a shape of air
Has entered the place; she goes away
And you know that little of her was there.
Yet it is only her heart you say?

You say that delicate flesh may ache
And blue veins throb and temples smart,
And yet, for trouble's intricate sake,
Nothing will splinter except the heart?

SAID TO A BIRD

What shall you do when the sun goes down?
Shake out your wing above the town.
Catch the redness of the west
Like a gladness against your breast;
Hold it like sorrow; this is done
To make you vibrant as the sun.
Offer yourself to space; a flake
Of darkened ether, you may wake
Breath in currents of long dead air.
And you shall *be*, and being there,
You will have shaped an instant to
The sleek mad contour that is you.

SUBMERGENCE

The only loneliness is the wind's,
The only sorrow is the sea's.
Why must a heart ache all life long
To learn such simple truths as these?

Lonely hours burn out like candles,
And sorrow is a leaf swept by;
But the wind is lonely forever and forever,
And the sea must hush an eternal cry.

WOMAN DEATH

Wash over her, wet light
Of this dissolving room.
Dusk smelling of night,
Lay on her placid gloom.
Wash over her; as waves push back the sands
Fold down her hands.

Many another rain
Of dusk has filled such walls;
Many a woman has lain
Submerged where the damp light falls,
Wanting her hands held down,
Finding it strange that they
Alone refuse to drown.

The mind after its day
Fills like an iron cup
With waters of the night.
The eyes wisely give up
The little they held of light.
Move over her, subdue her, Dark, until
Her hands are still.

Out of the east comes night;
From west, from north, from south,
Gathers the blackened light
To move against her mouth.
Many another has known
These four pressures of space,
Feeling her lips grow stone
And hollows curving her face,
And cared so little to feel.
Her light had never given

More than her dark might steal;
Then for this she had striven:
To feel the quiet moving on her hands
Like thin sea over sands.

Time gathers to break
In arrested thunder, gloom
Comes with thickness to make
Deep ocean of a room,
Comes to soothe and shape
The breathed-out breath.

Some who die escape
the rhythm of their death,
Some may die and know
Death as a broken song,
But a woman dies not so, not so;
A woman's death is long.

WORDS FOR WEEPING

If in your mind are hanging colors
Drenched with waters of a sleep
That might have woven living patterns,
Why not weep, why not weep?

If through your breast a heat is blowing
Like wind across a desert place,
Why not lift up pointed fingers
And lay them tightly on your face?

If sunlight is a sworded pleasure
At your throat, and if the blue
Of distance makes a cry of you,
Or if the night is but a darkness,
Why not weep a tear or two?

BREATH

This is the long, long song that is never sung,
What every lover of life has known as wine;
This that is speech forever on the tongue,
Forever missing shape of word, too fine
A passion to be tempered by a sound–
This that is honey of sun and the rain taste of the
     ground.

Little has ever been known of this or said,
Little need ever be said and little known;
This that falls away from the lips a thread,
Impalpable and glittering, is blown
And lost upon the elements like light–
This that is water of dawn and the sweet black ice of
     night.

Over the head Time poises like a wave,
Shielding an hour within its curving length,
An hour that has no thing to offer save
A curious pipe of madness and a strength–
This rhythm mixing lightly with the blood,
This tonic of dusk and leaves and drink of the moon's
     tart flood.

A Woman Ponders

My hands have uttered prayer.
They have been afraid
Of terror and despair.
My hands have uttered prayer.

My lips were more afraid
Of cowardice than pain.
They have not asked, nor made
A syllable of pain.

My lips have wrought a quiet
To bind them like a mesh,
A web that is a riot
Of silences… a quiet
That yet may snare the flesh.

THE TIRED MORTAL

I walk close to the blinding edge
Of night, but who would care to wander
In fields of dark with never the ledge,
Precipitous, to ponder?

Shunning now the prejudice
Of dissolution, lest it harm me,
I lean above the night that is
Profound enough to charm me.

In crucible that is the mind
I test night's utterness; such fire
Clarifies thought until I find
It veined with faint desire.

Other than this concern with night
I have no love. I am of those
Who, breathing too long in the light,
Cherish the dark repose.

ESTRANGED

I have broken with myself.
Sickened of my own breath, I turned;
As smoke away from flame that burned
The sweet of wood, I turned from self.

Now I am not to touch with hand,
Nor see with eye, nor hear with ear,
And holding nothing hotly dear,
Know only what I understand.

Over my old self I lean
Like a ray of shattered light,
While a small untroubled night
Widens in the space between.

ANY WOMAN

When there is nothing left but darkness
And the day is like a leaf
Fallen onto sodden grasses,
You have earned a subtle grief.

Never let them take it from you,
Never let them come and say:
Night is made of black gauze; moonlight
Blows the filmy dark away.

You have a right to know the thickness
Of the night upon your face,
To feel the inky blue of nothing
Drift like ashes out of space.

You have a right to lift your fingers
And stare in pity at your hands
That are the exquisite frail mirrors
Of all the mind misunderstands.

Your hand, potent in portrayal,
Falls of its own weight to rest
In a quiet curve of sorrow
On the beating of your breast.

BROKEN MOON

A broken moon is in the night,
And many shadows take to creeping
Like sulky panthers from the light...
Where shall I go for weeping?

Everything else is under the moon,
Even a graceful place to die in,
Chill with light as a dream of noon;
And there is a place to pray, to swoon,
But not the spot to cry in.

Under the moon there is no motion
But caught like ice, grows hard and sheer;
And eyes give up their trifling notion
Where sorrow is a cold devotion
That has no smallest tear.

The Unuttered

Griefs forsaken now and lonely
And hurt that is too proud for sound,
Cluster together and rhythm the darkness.
Never let their names be found,
Lest loose syllables be tightened
For utterance, lest they should form
In twisted meanings. Know them as blowing,
Know them for ungathered storm,
Their soft motion will be broken
To quiet, like the stir of a dove,
Like the dropped leaf. Let them move.
They will not elude your silence,
They will make good love.

The Silent Bard

What was my drink and meat
Is now my need.
Only is hunger sweet
To those who feed.

Only is thirsting dear
To those who know of wine,
For all they cry the sheer
Beauty of the vine.

I cleared the feast and learned
All was as before.
I am a beggar turned
From every door.

THE RELINQUISHER

You rid your blood of the sound of sea,
You hush your boasting heart and make
Your flesh as meek as your ash will be,
Cooling it well for your hands' hot sake,
Until your hands lie still together
Like one were stone and the other feather.

You press all beauty into word
So burning that it may accuse
Like a sorrow, like a sword.
You lose yourself to wear the shoes
Of sleep, and go where is no knowing
And the wind is blind with its own blowing.

If you have what life cannot take,
It is so nearly death's, no name
Will utter it. It is an ache
Grown numb: incurious love of flame
Upon the unseen hearth, the near
Beat of rain you do not hear.

DEATH DEFIED

Where is your tree could shade her
As life has done,
That covered her with black moon,
The colder for the sun?
What sodden dust, what carved stone,
Where now you bid her rest,
Could so cement her laughter,
So weigh upon her breast?

THE LOST HILL

I wonder if the grass is brown
And sharp with weeds as it used to be;
I wonder if the hill moves down
To break in rock before the sea.

I wonder whether others pass
That way, and if with racing feet
They feel the bitterness of grass
And find the harsh touch sweet.

And if they pause and standing there
Suddenly they grow tense and still,
Then turn from the sea and toss their hair
And laugh as children will.

CROSSED HEART

For sake of wind out of the south,
For sake of all the lean birds lost
In rhythm of their own long flying,
And for the sake of your hurt mouth
Closed forever on its crying,
Let your heart be crossed.

If you will lift a hand to make
A double motion, quick like breath,
Over your heart's uneven throbbing,
You will have done a thing for sake
Of that for which there is no sobbing,
Nor any hush of death.

Fearing the dazzle in your eyes,
Moments that wear you thin as moon
And make you exquisite with sighing,
Lay on your heart this light device,
Lest for that which knows no dying
You be dead too soon.

Song To Be Known Before Death

Laughter shapes a new love
In the mind now grown
Complacent with the sorrow
Of love that sleeps like stone.
Laughter is an arrow,
Blown as light is blown.

Laughter is the true love.
One by one by one,
First loves turn to trouble,
Grow wistful and are done.
But laughter is a bubble
Unmindful of the sun.

FLIGHT

A bird may curve across the sky—
A feather of dusk, a streak of song;
And save a space and a bird to fly
There may be nothing all day long.

Flying through a cloud-made place
A bird may tangle east and west,
Maddened with going, crushing space
With the arrow of its breast.

Though never wind nor motion bring
It back again from indefinite lands,
The thin blue shadow of its wing
May cross and cross above your hands.

SLEEP CHARM

Mistily my sleep comes down.
(What now of the brilliant sea?)
Mistily the silken brown
Darkness covers me.

Quietly my sleep draws near.
(What now of the wind's long flight?)
Quietly comes down the dear
Nothingness of night.

RIDDLE

Come, I would give you
A riddle to plague you.
What of the heaven
That spurs your sight—
That moves before you,
A shadow, moon-colored,
To blind and beckon,
A darkness, a light?

What of the heaven
Of which you know nothing
Save that it makes you
Timorous strength,
Save that it gives you
Silver for breathing,
Save that it leads you
Down the world's length?

The mind will not help you,
The mind's dry laughter
Will baffle and foil you;
Nor will the heart know.
Better to leave it
A riddle, to name it
Mist or a sunbeam,
Or dazzle of snow.

SLOW DEATH

You need no other death than this
Slow death that wears your heart away;
It is enough, the death that is
Your every night, your every day.

It is enough, the sun that slants
Across your breast, heavy as steel,
Leaving the rust of radiance
To shape a wound that will not heal.

Enough, the crystal at your lips,
Wasting you even as it lies—
Vibrant there before it slips
Away, torn from your mouth like cries.

There will be now, as fumes from wood,
A passing, yet no new death's care.
You will know only the frustrate mood
Of breath tarnished to color of air.

PROTEST

I

A quiet moves upon me.
It is not drifting snow.
Like snow it chills my mouth,
And brings my breathing low.
It moves like sand against me,
Cleaning, covering.
It is not sand; it is
Not anything.

II

Do lions fall down worn
And beautiful, to lie
In death that is but scorn
Of life, quite proud to die?

There is someone who would
Protest for fear her head
Be denied that lasting mood
Becoming to the dead.

III

They must walk ever where the wind
Curves like grain about their feet,
Never to stoop to pluck the wind
To learn if it be gold and sweet,
Never to have a stalk of wind
To carry in their hands like wheat.

HEARSAY

They say there are shadows
That wait for your hands,
Water-cool shadows
To cover your hands.

They say there is twilight
For eyes that are done
With piecing together
The colors of sun;
They say there is twilight
Kinder than sun.

They tell of the purple
Of time that will sweep
Over you, purple
Where you will sleep—
Purple time drifting
Like sand where you sleep.

Notes and References

Introduction

1. Quoted in Nicholl, p. 12.
2. Quoted in Franklin, p. 15.
3. Reverend William Wallace Youngson quoted in Franklin, pp. 47-48.
4. Quoted in Franklin, p. 30.
5. Ibid., p. 15.
6. Beth Bentley, in her ground-breaking introduction to the *Selected Poems*, was the first to clearly place Hall in relationship to the Georgian poets, and to establish her originality.
7. Although in her poems Hazel Hall dwelt on the circumstances of her confinement, she once confided to a friend, "I am not unmindful of my advantage." (Franklin 29)
8. Adrienne Rich, "Twenty-One Love Poems VII," in *The Dream of A Common Language*. (New York: Norton, 1978), p.28.
9. William Stanley Braithwaite, Boston *Transcript* (Sept. 6, 1921), p. 6.
10. Pearl Anderson. "Of Dreams and Stitches," *Poetry* (Nov. 1921), p. 100.
11. Quoted in Franklin, p. 22.
12. Three "Vignettes in Prose" appeared in *The Midland* (April 1, 1925): "The Boy Passes By," "On a Park Bench," and "The Red Hat." The first of these had been accepted before the author's death on May 11, 1924.

Curtains

title page
chintz (2). A brightly printed cotton fabric with designs of flowers, etc., in five or more colors.

Frames

springing (2). The pun alerts us to Hall's delight in language and linguistic play, even in the more despairing later poems.

Stairways

fancy (13). Used here and elsewhere in the sense of "imagination."

Counterpanes

Counterpanes. An old term for bedspread, here a patchwork quilt.

Late Winter

latticed sights (1). Divided, as by the narrow lathes subdividing a window.

A Child Dancing

feathery grace (10). Graceful movement.

Ecstasy

The concept of the universal mind? (11). "To the highly emotional and creative mind, such as my sister's was, religion was merged, along with other facts and phenomena of life, into an all-embracing viewpoint, gathering strength and reality because it was so merged." (Ruth Hall qtd. in Franklin 15).

Part Two: Needlework

A selection of the needlework poems appeared in *Poetry* (May, 1921) under the title "Repetitions."

Monograms

The relatively open form of this poem and others, particularly in the Needlework section of *Curtains*, recalls Hall's note to the reader in the frontis of the book: "In certain of these poems I have blended metrical and irregular rhythms in an attempt to contrast monotonous motion, presented in even measures, with interruption which is expressed in freer forms."

Mending

travesty (22). The word is used in its sense of a grotesque imitation of life.

A Baby's Dress

fagot-stitched bow-knots (5). An embroidery produced by gathering and tying threads into an hourglass or bow shape.

pasteboard (10). A flimsy cardboard made by pasting together layers of paper.

Plain Sewing

basted (6). Sewn with temporary loose stitches to hold in place prior to final sewing.

Lingerie

nainsook (4). A supple lightweight cotton fabric.

stiff bolt (5). A length of woven goods as it comes on a roll from the loom.

lawn (6). A plainwoven cotton fabric.

Filet Crochet

Filet crochet. A lace with geometric designs worked into a square-mesh ground (the "latticed net" of line 3).

lattice (11). Here the term refers to the framework of crossed lathes on which a rose would be trained.

Summer Sewing

dimities (1). Sheer cotton fabrics subtly checked or striped by the corded effect of raised threads.

marguerites (7). A white-rayed, yellow-centered, daisy-like flower.

Muslin (26). A plain cotton fabric often used for sheeting.

Habit

feather-stitch (8). An embroidery stitch in which a succession of branches extend alternately along a central stem.

Ripping

adventitious (8). Coming from another, outside source.

Made of Crêpe de Chine

Crêpe de Chine. A thin silken fabric of crinkled texture, having a waxy, luminous appearance.

After Embroidering

mercerized (1). A process in which, by treatment with caustic soda, a fabric is made lustrous, strong, and receptive to dyes.

never-flower (2). Imagined flower inspired by observing real tulips. (cf., *never-songs* in "Never," from *Cry of Time*).

Blossom-Time

censers (15). Covered incense burners swung on chains in religious rituals.

Walkers

dedication: To R.H.
Presumably her sister, Ruth Hall.

The Way She Walks

charactery (4). Sewn characters or symbols used to express thoughts.

Stranger

too tooled a track (2). As if the street were laid with railroad tracks, bearing the stranger inevitably forward.

Arraigned

arraigned (1). Accused and called forth to testify (cf., legal terminology in "Footfalls VI," "Self-Inquisition," and elsewhere).

Cry of Time

The Ravelling Tune

ravelling. Letting fall into a tangled mass.

Your Audience

Where minarets may justify the sun (10). Suggesting perhaps that the minarets, towers from which the summons to prayer is cried, represent a life-affirming faith.

The Sea

intrinsic (8). Essential or inherent, rather than merely apparent.

Every Day's Damocles

Damocles. A sword was suspended by a hair over the head of Damocles, the guest at a tyrant's banquet, to remind him of his peril. The image recurs in "Words for Weeping."

Breath

A curious pipe of madness (16). Reading "pipe" as a shrill sound, this seems to describe a high, keen, poetic utterance; a manic statement.

The Tired Mortal

crucible (9). A vessel in which substances are melted, or tested by fire.

Bibliography

Hall, Hazel. *Cry of Time*. New York: E.P. Dutton, 1928.
————. *Curtains*. New York: John Lane, 1921.
————. *Selected Poems*. Ed. Beth Bentley. Boise: Ahsahta, 1980.
————. *Walkers*. New York: Dodd, Mead, 1923.

Selected Sources

Andrews, Marcia S. "'When Silence Has Its Way With You': Hazel Hall (1886-1924)." In *Gender and Literary Voice*. Ed. Janet Todd. New York: Holmes & Meier, 1980. 87-107.

Bentley, Beth. Introduction. *Selected Poems by Hazel Hall*. Boise, ID: Ahsahta, 1980. iii-vii.

Franklin, Viola Price, ed. *A Tribute to Hazel Hall*. Caldwell, ID: Caxton, 1939.

Helle, Anita. "Looking for Hazel Hall–Between Lace, Lines, and 'Lingerie.'" *Northwest Review*, 35.1 (Winter 1997): 6-19.

Matthews, Eleanor H. "Hazel Hall." In *An Anthology of Northwest Writing: 1900-1950*. Ed. Michael Strelow. Eugene, OR: Northwest Review Books, 1979. 98-193.

Nicholl, Louise Townsend. Introduction. *Cry of Time*. New York: E.P. Dutton, 1928. 11-15.

Saul, George Brandon. "Hazel Hall: A Chronological List of Acknowledged Verses In the Periodicals." *Twentieth Century Literature*, 1 (April, 1955): 34-36.

————. "Wasted Flame? – A Note on Hazel Hall and Her Poetry." In *Quintet: Essays On Five American Women Poets*. The Hague, Netherlands: Mouton, 1967. 21-29.

Ward, Jean M., and Elaine A. Maveety, eds. *Pacific Northwest Women, 1815-1925: Lives, Memories, and Writings 1815-1925*. Corvallis, OR: Oregon State University Press, 1995. 283-85.

Index of Titles

Admonition Before Grief, 158
After Embroidering, 71
Ahead of Him, 93
And Either Way, 105
Answer, The, 37
Any Woman, 205
Apathy, 140
April Again, 106
Arraigned, 126
As She Passes, 131
At the Corner, 95
Audience to Poet, 155

Baby's Dress, A, 53
Bead Work, 50
Because of Jonquils, 16
Before Quiet, 153
Before Thought, 28
Bird at Dawn, 153
Blossom-Time, 75
Blue Hills, 162
Boy Went By, A, 80
Bracken, 122
Breath, 201
Broken Moon, 206
Buttonholes, 59

Captive, 26
Child Dancing, A, 18
Child Is Lost, A, 159
Child on the Street, A, 90
Circle, The, 38
Company, 18
Cooling Song, 193
Counterpanes, 14
Cowardice, 27
Cross-Stitch, 54
Crossed Heart, 211
Crowds, 96
Cry of Time, 150

Death Defied, 210
Defeat, 39
Destinations, 82
Disputed Tread, 86
Dubious Self, The, 176

Echoes, 32
Echoes of Her, 127
Ecstasy, 25
Eleventh Month, 178

Ephemera, 124
Epitaph for a Neighbor, 130
Estranged, 204
Every Day's Damocles, 184
Experienced Griever, 183

Falling Star, A, 29
Feet, 30
Filet Crochet, 57
Finished To-Night, 52
Flash, 31
Flight, 213
Floor of a Room, 8
Flower of Illusion, The, 120
Footfalls, 111
Footsteps, 6
For a Broken Needle, 164
For a Lost Grave, 191
For a Woman Grown Cold, 185
Foreboding, 78
Frames, 2

Good Walker, A, 101
Grey Veil, The, 36

Habit, 62
Hand in Sunlight, 154
Hand-Glass, The, 9
He Ran Past, 109
He Walked On, 125
He Walked on Leaves, 173
He Walks with His Chin in the Air,
    139
He Went By, 105
Health, 176
Hearsay, 217
Heat, 178
Heavy Threads, 58
Here Comes the Thief, 151
Hippity-Hopper, The, 128
His Eyes Are on the Ground, 135
Hours, 37
Hunger, 145
Hurrier, The, 125

Impartial Giver, The, 40
In April, 76
Inanimate, 71
Incantation, 167
Incidental, 118
Incontinence, 175
Inheritance, 163
Inland, 169

Instruction, 66
Intelligence, 179
Interim, 192
June Night, 3
Knitting Needles, 42
Late Hours, 48
Late Passer, A, 91
Late Sewing, 74
Late Winter, 16
Light Sleep, 177
Lingerie, 56
Listening Macaws, The, 69
Loneliness, 33
Long Day, The, 70
Lost Hill, The, 210
Made of Crêpe de Chine, 64
Maker of Songs, 190
Man Goes By, A, 121
Masks, 89
Maturity, 110
Measurements, 65
Mending, 49
Middle-Aged, 102
Monograms, 46
More Than Sound, 103
Moving Snow, 92
My Needle's Thread, 67
My Song, 35
Nakedness, 106
Never, 185
New Spring, 108
Night, 195
Night Silence, 13
Nobody Passes, 22
Noon, 194
October Chorus, 171
October Window, 123
Of Any Poet, 186
Of One Dead, 181
Old Man's Walk, An, 119
On the Street, 84
Passer, A, 99
Passers-by, 15
Patrician, The, 117
Paths, 62
Pedestrian, 136
Pity of It, The, 134
Plain Sewing, 55
Pleasantry, 175
Prayer Against Triteness, 133
Profit, 103
Protection, 138
Protest, 216
Proud Steed, The, 21
Pursuit, 100
Puzzled Stitches, 60
Rain, 180
Ravelling Tune, The, 156
Record, 35
Relinquisher, The, 209
Riddle, 214
Ripping, 63
Roads, 19
Room Upstairs, The, 20
Said to a Bird, 197
Sands, 41
Sanity, 141
Scarf, The, 183
Sea, The, 168
Seams, 51
Seasons, 5
Self Inquisition, 136
Sewing Hands, 55
Shadow-Bound, 28
Shadows, 23
Shawled, 91
Sighers, 94
Silence, 10
Silent Bard, The, 208
Singing, The, 99
Sleep, 182
Sleep Charm, 213
Slow Death, 215
Song To Be Known Before Death, 212
Songs for Dreams, 21
Songs To Be Said While Walking, 142
Stairways, 12
Stitches, 45
Stranger, 104
Submergence, 197
Summary, 148
Summer Sewing, 61
Sun Glamour, 3
Sunlight Through a Window, 34
Then the Wind Blew, 66
These Who Pass, 144
They Say Her Heart Is Broken, 196

They Who Walk in Moonlight, 147
They Will Come, 132
Thin Door, The, 137
Things That Grow, 11
Three Girls, 83
Three Songs for Sewing, 72
Through the Rain, 143
Tired Mortal, The, 203
To a Door, 7
To a Poet Who Said Too Much, 157
To All Quiet Persons, 165
To an Experienced Walker, 107
To an Indolent Woman, 152
To an Unpleased Passer, 146
To One Coming in Sight, 127
Today, 131
Tomorrow's Adventure, 181
Tract on Living, 187
Twilight, 24
Two Sewing, 68

Unseen, 17
Unuttered, The, 207

Very Old Woman, A, 81

Walker of Night, 140
Walkers at Dusk, 87
Walking, 97
Way She Walks, The, 88
Weeper in the Dark, 170
When There Is April, 77
Where Others Walk, 122
Whistler in the Night, A, 94
White Branches, 159
White Day's Death, 162
Wild Geese, 164
Winter Rest, 172
Woman Death, 198
Woman Ponders, A, 202
Words for Weeping, 200
World's Voice, The, 4

Your Audience, 160
Youth, 85

Index of First Lines

A bird may curve across the sky, 213
A broken moon is in the night, 206
A child with unmanageable feet, 18
A fibre of rain on a windowpane, 72
A footstep sounded from the street…,
    18
A great mouth, lean and grey, 13
A man may sigh as he goes by, 94
A needle has no memories, 71
A needle running in white crêpe de
    chine, 64
A quiet moves upon me, 216
A ray of jonquils thrills the grey, 16
After the song, there comes an hour,
    186
After you have passed, the silence, 103

Be thankful, weeper in the dark, for
    tears, 170
Beauty streamed into my hand, 34
Bright disks of sound, 94
Brown roads have been too muddy,
    127
Brown window-sill, you hold my all of
    skies, 2

Come, I would give you, 214
Come not here to listen, 171
Come out into the sunlight, come, 165
Crowds are passing on the street, 48
Cut a little opening, 59

Dawn paints quaint histories, 28
Day-long I hear life's sounds beat like
    the sea, 32
Did you have a yesterday, 136
Discomfort sweeps my quiet as a wind,
    27
Door, you stand in your darkened
    frame, 7
Dreams—and an old, old waking, 38
Dreams are eyes fixed on closed doors,
    35
Dusk with never a wing to make, 152

Even fine steel thinly made, 164

Far as near things are when sleep, 185
Feet, I am weary of your beat, 30
Feet that have walked in moving snow,
    92
For moments of this life's swift cycle
    made, 25

For sake of wind out of the south, 211
For this there is no sound, 150

Give me words to please my tongue, 167
Griefs forsaken now and lonely, 207

He goes whacking a stick, 80
He has a deft yet furtive way, 105
He has gone down the street, and I know he will not be back, 104
He is companioned secretly, 110
He is so bitterly concerned, 125
He lived because he found himself with breath, 130
He walks with a smile upon his lips, 93
He wore a cryptic sadness for the year, 173
Here are old things, 49
Here comes the thief, 151
His slow steps feel along the street, 119
How can I rid me, 118
How shall I keep April, 78

I am arraigned in listening to feet, 126
I am content with latticed sights, 16
I am holding up a mirror, 9
I am less of myself and more of the sun, 31
I am monogramming, 46
I am sewing out my sorrow, 70
I am stronger for having gone, 176
I am weary of your talk of sorrow, 192
I asked the watchful corners of a ceiling, 37
I can take mercerized cotton, 71
I did not see you, 109
I feel the leash-like straining of his motion, 140
I had forgotten the gesture of branches, 159
I have broken with myself, 204
I have curtained my window with filmy seeming, 1
I have envied, I have pitied, 138
I have known hours built like cities, 37
I have known life's hunger, 145
I have raised my hands to rain, 180
I have unleashed my hands, like hounds, 52
I have waked in the night to listen, 183

I hope I shall remember, 29
I know that you must come and go, 102
I like the things with roots that know the earth, 11
I make a band of filet crochet, 57
I plunge at the rearing hours, 21
I put one little slanting stitch, 54
I saw you go by, 128
I shall not be singing, 106
I walk close to the blinding edge, 203
I was sewing a seam one day, 51
I who have spent my hands in futile weaving, 40
I will make myself new thought, 14
I will think of water lilies, 153
I wonder as I watch you pass, 99
I wonder if the grass is brown, 210
If a wind blew up the street, 134
If culture had fluidity, 117
If I could look into your eyes, 141
If I listen shall I hear, 4
If in your mind are hanging colors, 200
If you will pass with your eyes before you, 127
Into my room to-night came June, 3
Is there a long hill, 146
Is this defeat then, after all, 39
It is made of finest linen, 53
It would be an unholy thing, 108

Last night when my work was done, 62
Laughter shapes a new love, 212
Lengths of lawn and dimities, 61
Let the day come out of the night, 142
Let the night weep on your hand, 158
Let them go by; I will not hear, 131
Life, be my pillow, 111
Life flings weariness over me, 36
Life in you is an incurious madness, 139
Life is my lover, 175
Life is such music in her ear, 122
Light that streams into the grass, 162
Low tide is the tide of sadness, 181

Many sewing days ago, 69
Mistily my sleep comes down, 213
My days are like sands; colourless, 41
My hands are motion; they cannot rest, 55

My hands have uttered prayer, 202
My hands that guide a needle, 66
My needle's thread is long and slow, 67
My song that was a sword is still, 35
My spirit is a captive bird, 26
My stitches, like the even tide of feet, 55
Needle, running in and out, 60
Needle, you make me remember things…, 62
Never by a window, 175
Never say of me, 183
No one has seen the beauty of the night, 195
No wonder they who pass all day, 96
Nobody passes on the street, 22
Not for any troubled reason, 172
Now I am Life's victim, 76
Now it is to be, 153
Now the time when winds may swoon, 178
Of course it's rather heavy, dear, 120
Often I am awaked from sleep to see, 17
Often I watch the walkers on the street, 84
Once when you walked through the spring, 107
One by one you follow, 140
One road leads out to the country-side, 19
One shadow on my wall, an intimate, 23
Over and over again I lose myself in sorrow, 163
Over and under, 45
Passers, pass me like the rain, 143
People walking up hill, 82
Perhaps his feet might choose in their new pride, 85
Perhaps the night wind will be tender, 159
Poet with the pointed breath, 155
Poet, your utterance becomes my breath, 160
Poets have talked too much about the sea, 168
Restless needle, where my beads, 50

Ripping, snipping, 63
Room just above me, 20
Sea, I have sworn never to sing of you, 169
She has a way of being glad, 106
She has beauty, she has youth, 131
She is as heavy as so much sand, 196
She knows some one is following her, 100
She passes by though long ago, 81
She sews the morning hours away, 156
She walks with a gravely conscious tread, 88
She wraps herself within herself, 91
Silence is the sound of footsteps, 10
Sleep came like rose petals falling on my pillow, 91
So long as there is April, 75
Some dreams that I have loved, 21
Something is waiting for him at the corner, 95
Sometimes when I am long alone, 33
Song is unrest, 99
Stitches running up a seam, 65
Strange that she can keep with ease, 90
Take strands of speech, faded and broken, 190
The day has brought me sun-loaned cheer, 3
The only loneliness is the wind's, 197
The street fills slowly with the thin, 87
The tops of trees rest my eyes, 66
The walls and windows of my room, 8
The wind is sewing with needles of rain, 68
There is a day for me when every footfall, 105
There is a quiet where you go at night, 182
There is a woman who makes my eye, 124
There is nothing new in what is said, 74
There should not be singing, 133
There was a throb of singing, 164
There were eyes before mine, 162
They are always looking for what they never find, 148

They are singing me never-songs again, 185

They cool their speech upon the tongue, 79

They have made a quiet for him, 181

They pass so close, the people on the street, 6

They say there are shadows, 217

They will come, at last they will come, who have not gone by, 132

This feather that is theirs to blow upon, 194

This is a quiet thing to say, 178

This is my hand I lift to you, 154

This is the long, long song that is never sung, 201

Three school girls pass this way each day, 83

Through hours woven of light and shade, 187

Time will light a candle at your head, 176

Tiptoeing twilight, 24

To-day my hands have been flattered, 56

Two lovely things, two green things, 193

Walk softly through the moonlight, 147

Walk, walker, that you may stamp out, 125

Wash over her, wet light, 198

What if it were true, People, 103

What shall you do when the sun goes down?, 197

What was my drink and meat, 208

Whatever my thought has spun, 179

When dawn was tipping like a sword, 184

When my great-grandmother died, 42

When the dawn unfolds like a bolt of ribbon, 58

When there is nothing left but darkness, 205

When you have walked where you would walk, 137

When you walk up a street you breast the air, 101

Where his sure feet pass, 121

Where is your tree could shade her, 210

Where she steps a whir, 86

Who is this who affects a window, 136

Who will be so quiet, 191

Who would fear death when there is April?, 77

Who would pity these who pass, 144

Why do I think of stairways, 12

Winter, spring, summer and fall, 5

Woman, if some one from your house had died, 122

Women who sing themselves to sleep, 177

Words drift between me and the street, 123

You—and you, Passer-by—and you, 15

You have tired me with your words, 157

You I will follow, 97

You need no other death than this, 215

You rid your blood of the sound of sea, 209

You wear your mask, 89

You, who walk with eyes upon the ground, 135

You whom the shadows beckoned, 28